GAME MISCONDUCT

INJURY, FANDOM, AND THE BUSINESS OF SPORT

NATHAN KALMAN-LAMB

FERNWOOD PUBLISHING
HALIFAX & WINNIPEG

Editing: Brenda Conroy
Cover design: Mike Carroll
Printed and bound in Canada

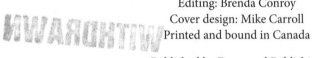

Published by Fernwood Publishing
32 Oceanvista Lane, Black Point, Nova Scotia, B0J 1B0
and 748 Broadway Avenue, Winnipeg, Manitoba, R3G 0X3
www.fernwoodpublishing.ca

Fernwood Publishing Company Limited gratefully acknowledges the financial support of the Government of Canada, the Manitoba Department of Culture, Heritage and Tourism under the Manitoba Publishers Marketing Assistance Program and the Province of Manitoba, through the Book Publishing Tax Credit, for our publishing program. We are pleased to work in partnership with the Province of Nova Scotia to develop and promote our creative industries for the benefit of all Nova Scotians. We acknowledge the support of the Canada Council for the Arts, which last year invested $153 million to bring the arts to Canadians throughout the country.

Library and Archives Canada Cataloguing in Publication

Kalman-Lamb, Nathan, 1983-, author
Game misconduct: injury, fandom, and the business of sport / Nathan Kalman-Lamb.

Includes bibliographical references and index.
Issued in print and electronic formats.
ISBN 978-1-77363-006-9 (softcover).—ISBN 978-1-77363-007-6 (EPUB).—
ISBN 978-1-77363-008-3 (Kindle)

1. Sports—Social aspects. 2. Sports—Economic aspects. 3. Athletes—Social conditions. 4. Athletes—Economic conditions. 5. Sports spectators.
I. Title.

GV706.5.K35 2018   796   C2017-907863-1
C2017-907864-X

CONTENTS

For all the athletes who work so that we may watch

ACKNOWLEDGEMENTS

I often think that this section is the most important part of any book. Every published text is, in at least minor ways, a combined effort, even if that fact is too seldom acknowledged. Certainly, *Game Misconduct* is fundamentally a work of collaboration.

As such, my most profound gratitude goes out to the individuals who so generously shared their stories with me: the eight former professional hockey players and eight sports fans. It is not an exaggeration to say that without their contributions, this book would have not been possible. I would also like to thank (but won't name in the interests of preserving anonymity) all of those who helped to put me in touch with the interviewees and others who ultimately chose not to be interviewed. My personal connections to professional hockey players are scant, so I relied a great deal on the benevolence of those who did have such connections and were generous in their willingness to share.

I owe a deep intellectual debt to my mentors at York University: To Anna Agathangelou and David McNally for teaching me about social reproduction, inspiring me with your own scholarship, and providing the encouragement this project required from its first inception in your respective classes to its ultimate publication. And, of course, above all, to Gamal Abdel-Shehid, always my teacher, mentor, collaborator, and friend. You enabled this project by giving me conviction in my work, a home in an alienating institution, and a constant sounding board for my ideas. So much of this book is owed to you.

Deeply sincere thanks to the great folks at Fernwood, who make the experience of publishing a book about as pleasant as I could possibly imagine it being. Thanks especially to Wayne Antony for his incredibly supportive editorial feedback; to Brenda Conroy for a really wonderful copy edit that managed to genuinely improve the accessibility and legibility of my prose; to Bev Rach for putting this project together and for putting up with my meddlesome queries; to Curran Faris for his efforts to make sure that this book has readers; and to the anonymous reviewer for a generous reading and insightful feedback.

I also feel a particular need to thank my colleagues in the Thompson Writing Program at Duke University for completely revitalizing my scholarly enthusiasm by providing the sort of supportive and collaborative intellectual environment I frankly did not believe could exist in the academy. I am particularly grateful to my cohort, and friends (alphabetically), Lisa Chinn, Mike Dimpfl, Marion Quirici, Sandra Sotelo-Miller, and Miranda Welsh for being so quick to embrace this Canadian radical, as well as to Jen Ansley, Brenda Baletti, Paolo Bocci, Sachelle Ford, Stefania Heim, Peter Pihos, and Amanda Pullum, among so very many other deeply appreciated colleagues, for their comradeship.

As this is a book fundamentally about labour, I also want to thank those I walked for months with on picket lines at York University in both 2008–09 and 2015 as part of CUPE 3903 — particularly my brother Gideon — as well as all those who laboured to form, bargain, and operate the Duke Faculty Union in an incredibly hostile anti-union environment in the U.S. South. My experiences as a union member have been incredibly formative in my analysis and general understanding of what it means to labour.

Finally, thanks are owed most of all to my family. To my little Elizabeth, for constantly keeping every aspect of my professional life in perspective, including this one. And, of course, to my partner and interlocutor in all things, Jen Selk, for her invaluable insight and expertise as an interviewer and for providing all the forms of social reproductive labour that give us — and this book — life.

CHAPTER 1

SPORT, SPECTACLE, AND SACRIFICE

On December 17, 2014, Chris Conte, player for the Chicago Bears of the National Football League, had this to say about the costs of athletic injury:

> Ever since I was a little kid, it's what I've wanted to do ... In college, I didn't even graduate school because my senior year, I honestly let school be a casualty to that because I knew I had one opportunity to make it to the NFL, and I put everything into that. And I felt school's something I could figure out later.
>
> As far as after football, who knows. My life will revolve around football to some point, but I'd rather have the experience of playing and, who knows, die 10, 15 years earlier than not be able to play in the NFL and live a long life. It's something I've wanted to do with my life and I wanted to accomplish. And I pretty much set my whole life up to accomplish that goal. So I don't really look toward my life after football because I'll figure things out when I get there and see how I am.[1]

About a month before, Steve Nash, player with the Los Angeles Lakers of the National Basketball Association, posted the following statement on Facebook after announcing that he would sit out the entire season:

> I definitely don't want to be a distraction, but I felt it best everyone heard from me in my own words.
>
> I have a ton of miles on my back. Three bulging disks (a tear

in one), stenosis of the nerve route and spondylolisthesis. I suffer from sciatica and after games I often can't sit in the car on the drive home, which has made for some interesting rides. Most nights I'm bothered by severe cramping in both calves while I sleep, a result of the same damn nerve routes, and the list goes on somewhat comically. That's what you deserve for playing over 1,300 NBA games. By no means do I tell you this for sympathy — especially since I see these ailments as badges of honour — but maybe I can bring some clarity.

I've always been one of the hardest workers in the game and I say that at the risk of what it assumes. The past 2 years I've worked like a dog to not only overcome these setbacks but to find the form that could lift up and inspire the fans in LA as my last chapter. Obviously it's been a disaster on both fronts but I've never worked harder, sacrificed more or faced such a difficult challenge mentally and emotionally.

I understand why some fans are disappointed. I haven't been able to play a lot of games or at the level we all wanted. Unfortunately that's a part of pro sports that happens every year on every team. I wish desperately it was different. I want to play more than anything in the world. I've lost an incredible amount of sleep over this disappointment.[2]

Years earlier, Professor Andrew Sparkes, of Leeds Beckett University in the U.K., who had been a standout teenage rugby player, wrote of his experiences after suffering developmental spinal stenosis as a consequence of his much less lucrative and celebrated athletic exploits:

Inhaling, I unfold my collapsible walking stick and begin to hobble. As my left foot hits the ground a searing, slashing pain, arcs from my lower back into my left buttock, left thigh, left calf muscle, and finally, into my foot. Right step-fine. Left step-stab. Right step-fine. Left step-stab. Left, left, left-stab, stab, stab … Stand still, lift left foot off the ground. Stand still, take all the weight on the right foot. Lean on my walking stick. Relief. Stand still. Move. Left step-stab. The world, my world, collapsing, into the left side of my lower body. I am my left limb. I am the space between pain and no pain. I stand still. I cannot take one more step. This is a world of stillness, slowness, impairment, disability, of otherness.[3]

Sparkes recounted what it was like listening to others describe watching him perform during his athletic prime: "They are celebrating a me I don't remember. A me I don't recall. Their applause is for a historical self, a ghost. Someone who was 'me' long ago. Things have changed. My body has changed. I have changed."

Chris Conte's disclosure is striking in two ways: he both acknowledges the extent of the physical sacrifices he has made *and* legitimizes those sacrifices. It is no surprise to anyone who participates in sport or to many who watch it that these games cause extensive bodily harm. Even so it is startling to hear this cost articulated in terms of losing "10, 15 years" of life. However, Conte's appraisal of the physical cost of sport is not unique. Professional athletes experience this reality every day. The second part of this equation is no easier to digest. Most people assume that Conte's willingness to sacrifice years off of his life is a product of the monetary rewards that he receives for playing. After all, it is a constant refrain that athletes are overpaid to an exorbitant degree. Conte's statement in no small measure tackles this assumption head-on from the outset. Although many athletes are paid more money than any individual is justly entitled to, a) this does not exempt them from being exploited as workers, b) only a relatively miniscule proportion of professional athletes receive outlandish sums, and c) they are compelled to make sacrifices that cannot be measured by money. Conte is not arguing that money justifies losing years of his life. He refers instead to a different motivation, the ambition he has had ever since he was a "little kid." Thus, he "pretty much set [his] whole life up to accomplish that goal." The game means something larger to Conte than dollars and cents and is something much more complicated to understand. This theme recurs again and again in the recollections of former pro athletes and is inextricably linked to their relationship with spectators.

Like Conte, Steve Nash refers to the tremendous damage suffered by his body over the course of his professional athletic career. Unlike Conte, Nash says that this toll — the sacrifice required of the athlete — may not be worthwhile. At a certain point the suffering his body is put through can no longer be justified. Yet, what is most remarkable about Nash's statement is who it is targeted at: his fans. He finds it necessary to explain his decision to those who follow and worship him. One might imagine that the intimate experience of bodily pain would be something he would prefer to keep private, yet he has chosen to share it with the world. In doing so, Nash acknowledges that the pro athlete's body does not exist in the private domain. His labour is not just in the public spotlight, it is *for* the public in fundamental ways. High performance professional athletes give up their bodies to the broader community — to the service of others.

If Conte instructs us about the physical cost of athletic labour and Nash indicates that the athlete's body is appropriated by the fan, Andrew Sparkes reveals what this costs the athletic labourer. Conte imagines what this cost will be, suggesting that he is willing, in the end, to lose years off of his life. Nash is less cavalier, disclosing that the toll on his body has already begun to significantly impact his quality of life. Sparkes provides us an even clearer window into physical harm that athletes endure. For Sparkes, pain has become "the world, my world." The implications of this go beyond his suffering (although that should not be minimized) — his entire sense of identity has changed. Where once his world was defined by the physical agency and mastery of the elite athlete, now it is "a world of stillness, slowness, impairment, disability, of otherness." Indeed, it is difficult even for him to recognize himself when he hears his past exploits being reported: "They are celebrating a me I don't remember." Sparkes brings us face-to-face with the full extent of the sacrifice made by the athletic labourer. The harm his body has experienced, the loss of physical ability, is the loss of the self he once was. This is a crisis that extends beyond pain alone. The full sacrifice the athletic worker makes has not yet been sufficiently discussed in popular or academic treatments of sport and injury.

This is not a wholly unique phenomenon. All workers in a capitalist society are in some way alienated. Workers, in contracting to sell their labour for a wage, lose connection with their capacity to work and with what they create. Workers' bodies become instruments for the will of the capitalist. Yet, while the athlete, like other workers, labours for the owner of the team (the capitalist), there is something different about the way in which the athlete's body is usurped. What Nash implies through his Facebook post is that another way his body is taken from him is that it becomes the temporary receptacle of the hopes and dreams of fans.

Nash apologizes to fans because he recognizes that his body has become the site of their investment — their hopes and dreams. His body is his own, of course, but for a time it has also, in a significant albeit ephemeral sense, been theirs.

Professional athletes are often understood in popular culture to be a highly privileged occupational group, owing largely to the fact that many workers are paid handsomely to play a game. In other words, professional athletes are typically viewed as the antithesis of exploited workers. This perspective, while seductive, ignores two facts: 1) many professional (minor league players, for instance) and revenue-producing (unpaid elite U.S. college sport) athletes are paid very little (and, in the cases of more well-compensated players, less than they are worth to the team) and 2) they are subject to highly unsafe working conditions. The former issue is clearly exploitation but so too is the latter, because professional sport is a workplace. In Canada, section 217.1 of the Criminal Code explicitly requires that "reasonable steps" be taken to prevent "bodily harm ... arising from ... work." Athletes are nevertheless subjected to unhealthy and unsafe working conditions as an inherent feature of their labour. This failure to apply worker safety regulations to athletic labour is clearly a form of exploitation. In fact, the violence that occurs in sport contributes to the popularity and profitability of the game. Indeed, this is precisely why professional athletes do not enjoy the protections supposedly guaranteed to all workers under Canadian law. Labour and employment lawyer Albert Kempf argues: "Hockey is sacred to all of our hearts as Canadians, more than any other sport, probably ... We don't want to mess up the game. Any province that attempted to go there [health and safety regulation] would probably feel a lot of pressure not to go there."[4] To understand why this is, we need to think more about how the business of professional sport works and what role injury plays in sport's popularity.

The sacrifice made by the athletic labourer is fundamental to the business of professional sport. This is not a complex argument from an economic standpoint. Every economy requires people to make purchases in order to generate profit. Capitalists make profit by investing money in a production process through the purchase of labour, raw materials, and machines. These "means of production" are transformed into commodities that are sold for more than the sum total of the means of production (this is because labourers are not paid as much as they deserve to be paid for the work they are doing, hence, exploitation). However, for capitalists to actually profit from their investment and the exploitation of workers, the commodities they produce must be purchased by consumers. If this happens, the capitalist invests this money back into production in order to continually and systematically generate increasing wealth. However, if the commodities produced in this manner *are not sold*, it becomes a loss for the capitalist. The productive cycle can only be completed through the purchase of the commodity by the consumer.

So what does all of this have to do with the business of professional sport? Well, it is really quite simple. For the owners of professional teams to earn a profit, they require consumers to purchase the commodities they produce: the athletic events they exhibit. That money may come from different sources. Ticket sales make up a decreasingly significant portion of total revenue. Nevertheless, whether it is the large rights contracts doled out by cable television companies or merchandising, the bottom line remains the same: the business of professional sport hinges on the desire of fans to invest their meaning and money in the teams they follow. Julian Ammirante puts it like this in his discussion of the business of the National Hockey League:

> This point bears repeating: the value to a sports organization — such as the NHL, the NFL, or any other sports franchise — of the services provided by the athletes it hires is derived from the demand sports fans exhibit for the events these inputs produce. All other things being equal, the payments athletes receive for their services are positively correlated with fans' demand for professional sporting events.[5]

The harm athletes experience in professional sport is not coincidental to the meaning that the spectators receive from watching, following, and investing in their team. It is a necessary part of what makes the commodity of professional sport desirable for the consuming fans. In fact, a spectator requires the athlete to be willing to make a sacrifice of his body in order for the fan to make the investment (emotional and financial) in the first place.* The experience and implications of athletic injury — and the full extent of exploitation inherent in professional sport — are directly connected to those of fans.

SPORT AS SOCIAL REPRODUCTION

In order to study the experiences of athletic workers in North America, we need to examine sport within the broader context of capitalism. However, instead of approaching this from the (typical) standpoint of the business of sport, or even a traditional Marxist analysis of exploitation (which focuses on the fact that workers are underpaid relative to the value they produce for the capitalist in the process of "productive" labour), I focus on how sport acts as a form of "social reproduction" — an invisible yet essential foundation for the wider economy. Capitalism constantly attempts to suppress wages to a subsistence level. Yet, *labour* is required for the worker to subsist. The work that goes into feeding, clothing, housing, and also caring for the next generation of workers is social reproductive labour. Social reproductive labour is the work required to satisfy basic human physical needs, such as food and shelter, and also basic human emotional, or affective, needs. This work must be done behind the scenes to produce a workforce capable of labouring for the capitalist economy. It is subject to its own brand of exploitation, for it is often labour that requires the sacrifice of a significant element of a worker's physical and emotional well-being in exchange for the well-being of another (worker). It has traditionally been performed by women in the home, and it is usually unpaid. It involves the reproduction of the worker's physical body *and* the worker's mental and emotional self.[6] This work can occur inside and outside the home by individuals who do not belong to the household. For example, the preparation of food is social reproductive labour, whether it is performed by a wife and mother (traditionally, not inherently — men are equally capable of this work), a servant, or a cook in a restaurant.[7]

Even paid social reproductive labour tends to have a high cost for the labourer that is not fully remunerated. For instance, the domestic labourer

---

*   I use "his" in this book because this is a study of the business of men's professional hockey. It may in many ways apply directly to the experience of women in professional sport, but given that women's professional sport is a less lucrative business, I make no such assumptions and thus stick to the masculine pronoun for the sake of specificity, not universality.

can, through the very fact of her employment in this form of work (again, this is typically gendered work), reproduce identity for her employer. Bridget Anderson writes that the paid domestic worker reproduces "the female employer's status (middle-class, non-labourer, clean) in contrast to herself (worker, degraded, dirty)."[8] The female employer does so through the purchase of the employee's "personhood," not just her labour-power. Beyond allowing for survival/subsistence, domestic labour thus also reproduces status — that is identity, power, and affect/emotion — within social relations. Social reproductive labour reproduces (figuratively) hearts and minds as well as bodies at the very real but uncompensated cost of a worker's fundamental well-being. In short, social reproductive labour re-humanizes some for their role in the capitalist system, while simultaneously dehumanizing those who perform it. Most workers in paid social reproductive sectors (for instance, domestic and even sex work) are typically subject to violence and insecurity, and thus dehumanization.[9] These workers are also often guided in their choice of profession by a level of economic constraint — and thus a lack of choice in the truest sense of the word. Both of these characteristics are often, although not always, more extreme than those facing professional athletes. Nevertheless, much can be learned about athletic labour from examining the social reproductive dynamics of these types of work.

FANDOM AS AN IMAGINED COMMUNITY

Up to this point, we have only been looking at one side of social reproductive labour: those who perform the work. However, the entire premise of social reproduction is that someone is being reproduced. With regard to pro sports, this is where the fan enters the equation. Spectatorship is a process of identity formation. Membership in a community of fans is a choice, even though it is made in the context of neoliberal capitalism. This context is important to understanding the imperative many feel to belong to communities of sports spectatorship. Neoliberal capitalism is characterized in large part by the isolation and alienation of people within a system that relentlessly seeks to individualize them as market actors. This arrangement of social relations produces a powerful desire (need?) for meaningful relationships and human connection that are not mediated by economic exchange. In short, it produces a ravenous hunger for community in whatever guise it might appear, including some forms that are more symbolic than "real" — for example, sports fandom. Professional sport has flourished because it offers something that is particularly coveted in a capitalist context: the possibility of meaning in the form of community.

Collective identity formation through fandom is a form of what Benedict Anderson calls an "imagined community."[10] This refers to a community formed by a group of people who shares norms and cultural characteristics, even if the individuals involved have no tangible relationship to one another. This stands in stark contrast to communities of athletes, for the *team* is perhaps one of the most "real" communities. An imagined community of fans is a spectacular (meaning relating to spectacle) community in that it offers people an image of the community they desire. This form of community may actually inhibit the development of real, tangible relationships between people. Instead, it unites people through a common allegiance to symbolic objects, like uniforms, memorabilia, and the like. Indeed, the imagined community is produced through what Paul Gilroy calls "logo-solidarity": the idea that a visual image can represent the existence of a community in the place of the actual human connections and networks we would conventionally expect to be its foundation.[11] Logo-solidarity is a useful notion for understanding how the imagined community of fandom is formulated and maintained. If fans gave serious thought to the fact that the team they support is a business designed to extract as much of their hard-earned income as possible, and if they reflected on how irrational it is to passionately exhort individuals nominally representing a certain area, even though those individuals may not even live there, it would be difficult to sustain the experience of fandom. Thus, the sense of meaning and belonging acquired through fandom is frequently fleeting. Because it is often not founded on actual social relationships, it must be renewed over and over again through the acquisition of commodities such as jerseys and caps.

THE SACRIFICIAL ARENA

The social reproductive dimensions of athletic labour — the ways in which athletic labour provides community and meaning for fans — are in sync with the demands of capitalism. The success of professional sport in satiating the worker's need for emotional subsistence helps sustain the capitalist system, which is nourished by the robust labour-power of workers. A worker who feels emotionally despondent will not be equipped to provide the maximum labour-power a capitalist requires in order to produce the largest possible profit. This is an increasing problem for capitalism as it comes to rely more and more on labour in the service sector — labour based around exhaustingly artificial interpersonal relations of exchange — to generate the ever-larger markets the system requires in order to continually produce profit. Workers in the service sector and others often experience burnout or lose the capacity to feel emotion.[12] This makes it difficult or impossible for them to perform their work and live full emotional lives. More generally, the satisfaction of "sexuality" and "nurturance" "is just as basic to the functioning of human society as is the satisfaction of the material needs of hunger and physical security."[13] Thus, workers require fulfillment of their emotional needs in order to be fully ready to work. Neoliberal capitalism produces societies in which each of us is increasingly isolated. This is all the more essential in a context where people interact with screens as much or more than one another.[14] For any of us to get up, go to work, and provide maximum labour-power, we must be refreshed emotionally and psychologically, as well as physically. Yet, the work of this emotional labour places exceptional and perhaps unquantifiable demands on those who perform it. It asks them to give something fundamental of themselves in order to refresh another.

Social reproductive work can be profoundly costly to those who do it. This cost cannot simply be measured in terms of lost wages, as with other forms of capitalist labour. Rather, it is a personal sacrifice of the body through injury, both acute and chronic, that athletes are compelled to make because of the social reproductive aspects of their work. This harm can accumulate to the point at which it becomes debilitating, particularly once athletic careers end. The damage is not simply physical; it can also lead to a crisis of identity, as most athletes understand themselves as people with extraordinary physical capacities (as in the case of Andrew Sparkes). It is in this sense that violence — defined broadly as physical and mental harm — is not an incidental part of athletic labour, including in sports that are not usually considered violent (tennis, baseball, etc.). The sacrifice athletes must make of opening themselves up to harm in their occupational life fuels the incredible popularity of professional sport. It is precisely *because* athletes are willing to sacrifice themselves on behalf of the team that the imagined community becomes meaningful and real for the fan, for imagined communities are always premised on the idea that its members will, as Anderson puts it, "willingly … die for such limited imaginings."[15] Fans require players to persevere through the generalized violence of professional sport rather than rejecting it by retiring, refusing to play, or demonstrating a general lack of passion or intensity. A refusal would signify to the fan the artifice of the imagined community of fandom. It is little wonder that on the rare occasion that such a refusal does occur, the response of fans is unsparingly venomous. Spectators from Toronto will recall the merciless about-face of Toronto Raptors fans towards their one-time hero Vince Carter when he chose to protect his body rather than play through injury at all costs.* A fuller accounting of the exploitative dimensions of athletic labour must consider the fact that the player offers up his entire self to reproduce the fan, yet is compensated only for his productive labour.

Sport is a form of social reproductive work in that the body of the athlete becomes a vessel for the meaning that sustains the business, the political economy, of sport. The sacrifice, or potential sacrifice, of the athlete's body is a significant element of the appeal of spectator sport, for it sets the stakes high enough to justify emotional and economic investment. Athletes must be willing to sacrifice their bodies in order to sustain the fiction of the imagined communities of sports fandom. By providing something for fans to invest meaning in and a basis on which to form the communities they need to compensate for the dehumanizing effects of capitalism, athletes become part of the reproduction of the spectator's emotional capacity to serve as a worker. This work allows the spectator to combat the isolation and alienation that make it difficult to provide the system with the optimal productive work it demands. In other words, athletic labour provides an important part, although not the only part, of the emotional sustenance fans need. There is a tremendous cost to the athlete who performs this social reproductive labour. The body becomes so damaged that it is unlikely to ever fully recover its former capacities. The toll is also mental/emotional, for the loss of the physical capabilities

---

* A quick Google search yields a Reddit thread entitled "Why do people hate Vince Carter" and an article from NBCSports.com (Feldman, 2014, November 19) crediting the "ugly end" of his "tenure in Toronto" to the fact that "he let his effort slip." Significantly, there is no mention in that piece of the myriad injuries he suffered, including injuries to his knee that would require surgery (Campigotto, 2014, November 19).

that once served as the foundation for the athlete's identity is profoundly dispiriting.

INJURY EPIDEMIC

Injury is a structural feature of team spectator sport. It validates a spectator's investment by demonstrating how much is at stake through the very fact that violence, pain, and injury are literally enacted upon the bodies that participate. One indication of this is in the rate of injury in games versus practices. A study of six NHL seasons indicates that 88.7 percent of injuries occur in games rather than practices.[16] While this discrepancy may reflect the fact that teams have an incentive not to lose players to injury in practices from the perspective of their ability to win games, actual games are the time when the play of players is observed by spectators who pay to see it. Athletic labour only has social reproductive potential when it is performed in front of those it is tasked with reproducing: fans.

With regard to the athletes I interviewed for this book, not a single one of them was recruited because he had experienced injury, yet each recounted a considerable history with injury. The number of participants in this study was not large enough to allow us to come to definitive conclusions about the frequency of injury in hockey or sport more broadly, but others have looked at this question. In regard to the NHL (the highest level of professional hockey), one study tracked an average of 857 players per year over the six-year period from 2006–07 to 2011–12 and found an average of 864 on-ice time-loss injuries per year.[17] This means that, on average, every player experiences at least one injury a season that requires them to miss playing time. (This is a significant bar because there is a huge incentive for the team to play players through injuries.) Given this rate, over a lengthy career, all players will accumulate a large number of injuries. Injury is simply a fact of professional hockey, just as it is a fact of athletic labour in general. Indeed, a review of research on injury incidence in popular contact sports found that the rate of injury in ice hockey for defenders (the position most likely to be injured) was the lowest of any sport on a list that also included bull riding, boxing, rugby, professional roller hockey, football, and Asian soccer.[18] It is also noteworthy that the highest percentage of injuries to any part of the body was to the head, at 17 percent. This was followed by the thigh, at 14 percent, and then the knee and shoulder, both at 12 percent.

The especially high incidence of injuries to the head is particularly significant given the proliferation of research on head trauma, specifically concussions. It has been estimated that the total number of sports-related concussions per year in the U.S. is somewhere between 1.6 and 3.8 million.[19] This number is so uncertain because most concussions are not reported. Although all concussions are dangerous, the greatest risk comes from repetitive injury. In cases of a single concussion, no more than 15 percent of people experience symptoms after a year. Of course, professional athletes in contact sports are extremely likely to experience repeated concussions. The prognosis for those who fall into this category is much different: "Recent research results have demonstrated neuropathologic evidence of (chronic traumatic encephalopathy) CTE in participants of many sports outside of boxing, including American football, professional hockey, and professional wrestling." CTE symptoms include "impairments in cognition … , mood … , and behaviour." These mood and behavioural symptoms include "depressed mood and/or apathy, emotional instability, suicidal ideation and behaviour, and problems with impulse control, especially having a 'short fuse.' Substance abuse (sometimes fatal) and suicide are not uncommon." As the condition worsens, the effects are especially felt in terms of memory impairment, ability to plan and organize, language difficulties, aggression, and apathy. There is still no broad enough study on who gets it, but risk factors appear to be associated with more severe and more frequent traumas. The health implications of concussions — principally the onset of CTE — are significant and, at least in the context of American football, particularly professional football, this consequence is disturbingly pervasive. A 2017 study published in the *Journal of the American Medical Association* found evidence of CTE in the donated brains of 177 of 202 former football players, including 110 of 111 former National Football League players. Of the 177 brains containing evidence of CTE, 133 were severe cases and 44 mild.[20] It is clear from the reports of former professional hockey players that concussions are a nearly unavoidable part of their sport as well.

ATHLETIC LABOUR AND FANDOM

This book examines how athletes and spectators in the world of professional sport experience and make meaning out of injury, fandom, and the business of sport. I provide lengthy excerpts of players' and fans' testimony rather than paraphrasing, synthesizing, or quantifying so that readers have a transparent window into the ways in which athletes and spectators experience professional sport. Both players and fans speak to the ways in which professional sport functions as social reproductive labour and reveal what this labour does *to* players and *for* fans. These descriptions suggest that athletic labour is more integral to the capitalist system than we might have thought and also that this has profoundly harmful consequences for the players, whose labour and sacrifice sustains an entire system of compensatory meaning in the form of imagined community.

Hockey players understand their relation to the broader economy in terms of the way they are subjected to the forces of labour market competition. They are under no illusions about the fact that their work produces value for ownership through commodification, exploitation, and alienation. Yet, their comments also suggest that athletic labour functions within the broader capitalist system as social reproductive labour that generates meaning for fans. It is clear in the stories of players that they are conscious to varying degrees that this second level of exploitation is occurring. Although they do not use the language of social reproduction, they are highly aware of the significance of their relationship to fans in the business of hockey. Indeed, this awareness of the expectations of fans has a tangible impact on the ways in which they play and the decisions they make about pain and injury. This is a question of economic necessity, but it is also a function of a shared understanding between players and fans that the athletes are entrusted with a disproportionately large investment of meaning by spectators. This investment is profound — it elevates players to the status of heroes and fans to membership in the community of the team. Fans construct meaning and develop an imagined community through their experiences of spectatorship in ways that place expectations and demands on players. Fans turn to sport because they are able to experience camaraderie, purpose, excitement, and even exhilaration that allows them to transcend their everyday existence for a few hours and become part of something larger than themselves.

Whereas athletes view their labour as fundamentally linked to a broader political economy, spectators tend to reject this notion, portraying sport as a site of play and inherent meaning and pleasure unsullied by the realm of capital. This is not at all surprising when we consider that the meaning of the imagined community of fandom is linked to an understanding that the community is profoundly *real*, not merely the construct of corporate capital. However, given its tenuous foundation in a game, the imagined community of fandom requires constant reinforcement through team-related merchandise and superstitions and rituals. It also requires athletes to prove its validity through a willingness to sacrifice their bodies in the service of their team. These sacrifices provide the ultimate evidence that the imagined community is worthy of the fans' passion and investment.

Fandom is premised on a desire among those who participate for connection and community. The team serves as a common site of investment that brings together disparate and atomized individuals. While participants are connected by a passion for sport, it is the community of fandom itself that satiates their more profound needs and links them together in lasting ways. Yet, this imagined connection is premised on the logic that the team a fan belongs to is always counterpoised against an antagonist. Fandom via the imagined community thus often takes a profoundly antisocial and even gendered form.

Professional athletes experience a range of consequences for the social reproductive role they assume through their labour. In fact, the very task of playing the part of a social reproductive labourer is something that feels deeply unnatural and straining for many. Moreover, the act of creating meaning and purpose for multitudes of spectators has a dark side, for in the end the process leaves most players feeling empty and discarded. Perhaps most significantly, the ubiquity of injury — which plays such an important part in generating meaning for spectators — leaves athletic labourers struggling with physical and emotional damage long after their careers are over.

It may be possible to participate in sporting cultures without becoming complicit in the current dehumanization of both athletes and specta-tors. What this requires is a rapprochement between players and fans. Capitalism systematically separates, distances, and commodifies indi-viduals, destroying the bonds of human connection and community. The solution to this dehumanizing social arrangement is not spectacular surrogate forms of fabricated community predicated on athletic sacrifice, but rather, the re-humanization of the relationship between fan and player. It is through an acknowledgement of shared humanity, pain, and passion that more authentic and humanely productive forms of community are possible. This is not simply idealism. During the 2011 National Basketball

Association lockout, players and fans came together to organize their own version of elite athletic performance. That experience transcended anything professional athletic spectacle had ever previously offered for at least some of the players and fans who participated. It remains a beacon for how sport might be resistant to rather than complicit with the dehumanizing and totalizing demands of capital.

Although this book is largely about hockey, the phenomena it explores are not in most ways unique to hockey culture. This is why I begin it with the voices of athletes who do not play hockey, and I end it by turning to some of the political possibilities raised by basketball culture. Fandom and labour, desire for meaning and sacrifice, are fundamental characteristics of professional sport. I had the privilege and opportunity to explore them in the context of hockey. It is the structural and ideological contexts that make experiences such as those described by Chris Conte, Steve Nash, and Andrew Sparkes, as well as the eight hockey players I interviewed, possible and similar. It is only by bringing athletes' voices into conversation with the ideas and experiences of spectators that we can begin to grasp why athletic labour requires such incredible sacrifice from athletes, who must be willing to potentially concede "10, 15 years" off of their lives. Above all, the question is whether this sacrifice is a necessary part of professional sport and, if so why. It is in the words and experiences of athletes and spectators themselves that we find the richest and most provocative answers.

CHAPTER 2

HOCKEY PLAYERS TALK ABOUT THEIR WORK

Professional hockey players know that their work produces value and profits for team and league owners. They clearly see their own labour as a commodity (something to be bought and sold). Consequently, they experience many of the hardships associated with work in a capitalist system, notably pressures from the large group of underemployed and unemployed players and lack of control over the conditions of their labour. Yet, athletic labour is not the same as most other work; it is not merely productive labour. It also functions as social reproductive labour — it generates the meaning fans crave and around which they can form community.

It is at this social level that the greatest sacrifices are required of players. Yet, it is clear in their talking about it that they are not totally or always aware of this second kind of exploitation. However, in terms of the business and economics of professional sport, although they may not put it in these terms, players are acutely conscious of the significance of their relationship to fans. The relationship with fans affects both the way that players play and the decisions they make to play through pain and injury. At times players consciously play for fans, knowingly giving them what they need. This is only partly owing to the economic conditions. It is also partly borne of a relationship in which fans invest meaning in players and players mirror that meaning back to them. In this way, players elevate themselves to the status of heroes/symbols and fans to membership in the team.

Even as this happens, players are always aware that fans do not understand the extent to which their "play" is arduous work. They realize that fans do not know what they are putting their bodies through and the sacrifices that they are making for them. Athletes labour in order to produce a particular type of product: meaning for fans. This process is alienating, but it is also absorbing and temporarily empowering for athletes. The athlete produces a commodity beyond just entertainment. Athletes produce something that the spectator takes away from the game, something that nourishes and revitalizes them.

INTERVIEWING HOCKEY PLAYERS

I decided to interview athletes rather focus on the endless archive of athlete interviews compiled by the media because the persona presented by professional athletes to the media is highly constrained by considerations outside the questions themselves. This assumption is underlined by Luc, one of the players I spoke with:

> Answering a question the wrong way can just make something escalate, something that now will big time affect the team and ... these people are trying to sell newspapers and they're doing that on your back. So it's something that you really have to deal with as an athlete and it's not always fun.

Indeed, this is not merely a question of personal self-preservation. As another player, Curtis, makes clear, players are explicitly trained to withhold candour during media interviews:

> You went into media mode and you answered the question without really saying anything. We were coached and we were told specifically ... not to give up too much information, not to say anything that would be posted on the opponents' wall as motivation for them. So there is sort of a code that when you interact with media ... and the guys are doing it better today than ever, you answer the questions without saying anything at all.

For this reason, and because some of the issues I am interested in are sensitive and personal, I guaranteed anonymity to the players I interviewed. This allowed the individuals I spoke with to explore areas they were not often asked to discuss in the media, and that would yield more fruitful insights into the experience of high performance athletes.

Anonymity is integral to the story told here. The names of the players have been changed, and potential identifying characteristics have also been altered.

Because of the ease of connections and prevalence of professional hockey players in Canada, I decided to focus this research on hockey players and fans. This story nevertheless provides a clear window into these same dynamics in other professional sports that put a toll on the body. I had originally considered interviewing both current and former players in order to gauge whether their attitudes changed over time, but it proved difficult to make contact with current players because of their time constraints. In any case, former players are likely to have a greater degree of perspective that allows them to situate their careers in the broader context of their lives as a whole. In fact, I suspect that current players may have too great an investment in the norms of professional hockey to challenge them. After all, it is difficult to imagine how it would be possible to fully acknowledge one's own exploitation and the physical harm it was causing and then to continue performing the activity.

Players I talked to come from a range of positions in professional hockey, from the major juniors to Europe to the NHL. The wide range of contextual factors limits making too many and too broad generalizations, but this breadth testifies to the relevance of the themes in question. In terms of diversity, there were no professional female athletes interviewed for this project. This is connected to the significance of hockey as a business for the larger argument of this book, as women's professional hockey has not reached the same scale. Nevertheless, it would have been valuable to talk to some professional female athletes. I was also interested in hearing about the experiences of non-white and white players alike. This was limited by my connections, the pervasive whiteness of professional hockey and the decision of players I approached. Two players who identified as non-white did share their experiences as part of this project.

I was born in Toronto and I am a long-time fan and follower of most sports. This provides me with a high comfort level both in discussing sport-related issues and with locker room dynamics and jocularity. With respect to the athletes I spoke to (in person, at least), I believe that my presentation as a white man, as well as my familiarity with sport, contributed to a relatively easy chemistry and comfort level. I come across as someone who is expected to be in a hockey locker room.

Lawrence

Lawrence is a forty-six-year-old Canadian-born man of English and Scottish descent. He had a lengthy career in the NHL. Although Lawrence was a goal-scorer in his junior hockey days, he became an "enforcer" in the NHL.

Vasil

Vasil is a thirty-nine-year-old Canadian-born man of Macedonian descent. He identifies as Muslim but says that it is not a significant part of his identity. Vasil is a former professional hockey player who had a career as a goaltender in the AHL (American Hockey League) and attended a number of NHL training camps, although he never played in the NHL.

Sean

Sean is a thirty-seven-year-old Canadian-born man of Irish descent who identifies with his Irish-Catholic upbringing. He is a former professional hockey player who played a lengthy professional career in the United Kingdom and United States. He played as a "stay at home" defenceman.

Luc

Luc is a forty-nine-year-old Canadian-born man of French-Canadian descent. He is a former professional hockey player who had a lengthy career in the NHL. Early in his career he was a scoring-focused offensive player. As his career advanced, due to injuries, he became a "vet," relied upon more for his experience and two-way play.

Darin

Darin is a forty-two-year-old Canadian-born man of Danish descent. He is a former professional hockey player who split a lengthy career between the AHL and NHL. Darin's role for the duration of his career was as an enforcer, tasked with protecting the other players on his team.

Chris

Chris is a twenty-five-year-old Canadian-born man of Jewish and English descent who consciously identifies as Jewish in order to subvert stereotypes. He is a former semi-professional hockey player who played for a number of years in the OHL. His role on the team during that time was as a third- or fourth-line grinder, a scoring player relatively low on the depth chart.

James

James is a thirty-two-year-old Canadian-born man who identifies as having a multi-racial heritage. He is a former professional hockey player and goaltender who played a lengthy career in the AHL and NHL.

Curtis

Curtis is a forty-two-year-old man who identifies as Canadian. He is a former professional player who played in the NHL and AHL. Curtis was drafted as an offensive defenceman — a role he had played as a junior player — but was converted to an enforcer in professional hockey, a role he never found to be comfortable.

PROFESSIONAL SPORT AS WORK

It is something of a cliché to assert that professional athletes are paid too much money to play games. There are myriad problems with this statement, notably the fact that these games are perhaps the most popular form of culture in North American society and that professional players are working as much as (or more than) they are playing. My interest is in how players understand what they do as work, just like so many other jobs.

Take James for instance. When asked about whether he felt as if he was playing a role or being himself when he played hockey in front of fans or interacted with them, he responded, "I wasn't really too concerned about fans or what anyone thought of me. I was just trying to get my job done." Here, then, we begin with a matter-of-fact statement about the everyday nature of athletic labour. It is simply a job to be done, not a dream or game. It was work and he did it. Did he notice whether or not spectators had expectations of him as an athlete? "Yeah, for sure, they expect certain things, they expect you to talk to them. I mean, little kids are one thing, but once you got with the older people, it's just, this is a little too much." Again, he dispels the common-sense notion that athletic labour and the celebrity that accompanies it are anything but a job. He acknowledges a basic level of responsibility to children but delegitimizes the obligations he was compelled to honour for adult fans. It is in the next exchange with me that he reveals the full extent of his attitudes toward athletic work:

> James: *I mean, I didn't really like playing, so …*
>
> Nathan: *Can you say that again?*

James: *I didn't really like playing, so …*

Nathan: *Oh? Why not? Can you tell me more about that?*

James: *It was … I don't know, I couldn't really put my finger on why, it just became a job, right, it's been a job for me since I was fifteen, sixteen … When I was in the* OHL, *it was like, "This is my job, this is what I have to do." And, you just kind of have the expectations you're gonna play in the* NHL *and if I'm gonna play in the* NHL, *then I'm gonna keep doing it, but it wasn't like you were playing for fun type of thing.*

Nathan: *And would you say that the reason you were doing it was because you had the athleticism and the skill that you could …*

James: *Yeah, I could get paid a lot of money to do it … I mean, I think most of the guys I played with wouldn't do it for free.*

Nathan: *Okay, and would you want to keep playing hockey now as a leisure activity on the side, obviously, of an occupation, but is it something you find fun to go out and do?*

James: *No, I haven't gotten on the ice once since I stopped, well, once or twice with my junior team just because they wanted me out there, but I'm not gonna play men's league or do any of that stuff.*

The first striking aspect of this exchange is actually not what James has to say, but my response. When he tells me that he didn't really like to play at all, I initially ask him to repeat this answer — betraying my disbelief — and then am unable to conceal my surprise. Despite my own critical attitudes towards sport and its indifference towards and commodification of athletic bodies, I have clearly also internalized the view that sport is play. The fact that I seem to have been caught off-guard also speaks to my expectations. I am in part taken aback because James's answer does not line up with the answers of most of the other players I spoke with. While they tended to feel a level of investment in the ideology that athletic success was inherently meaningful, much like fans, James has obviously resisted this narrative.

It is clear that James is conscious that athletic labour is in no way distinct from other kinds of work. He explicitly states that he has not felt it was a game since he was a teenager, since he has been paid to play. From the moment that his performance became a commodity, it evidently lost its appeal for him to such an extent that he is no longer interested in playing for leisure. James appears to have been alienated from his work in much the same way as most other workers. Because he was being paid to play for a team owned by someone else for the satisfaction of others, he stopped feeling a "playful" connection to the game. This in turn changed the way that he sees hockey in general. It became mechanical and work-like and thus holds little interest for him. Although he is obviously not able to speak for other players, it is interesting to hear him say, "most of the guys [he] played with wouldn't do it for free." While most players do tend to acknowledge that playing professional hockey is something of a dream, this does not preclude a simultaneous sense of alienation. Perhaps there is an abstract satisfaction to having achieved the goal of making the NHL even as that fulfilment is debased through the daily rigours of the job.

James's understanding of athletic work is echoed by Vasil:

> After my eighth year of professional hockey, I had an agent that ran a goalie school and the guy that ran that goalie school wanted to start a new goalie school. So myself and him started [our school]. And, that summer, when we talked about it, I was thinking about still playing and playing Europe, but I just had my first child, and thinking about family and future, and to be honest with you, one day you could be a really good hockey player and the next day you can't, so ... contracts can come and go, so having a steady job was in the back of my mind and I was twenty-nine years old and a future for my family and if I went over to Europe, there's really no health coverage and all that. So you know, people don't realize that. Yeah, it's a great job and it's fun and all that, but they don't know the little things that happen to players that, if you don't play well, or things like that, and you could be gone.

While his overall attitude towards professional hockey remains favourable, it is evident that beneath this veneer are significant concerns about the life of a professional player. He elected to stop playing the game because of the constant pressures of other players vying to take his job and the precarious state of his health as a result of the game. He implicitly references the myth that athletic labour is a dream ("Yeah, it's a great job and it's fun and all that") and then refutes it, suggesting that most fans don't realize how arduous the job really is.

Although only a couple of the athletes spoke explicitly about the way in which their labour was alienated, the constant pressure they faced from a ceaseless flow of aspiring professional players was a persistent theme. A surplus population of workers — sometimes called the industrial reserve army — who are willing and able to work but currently find themselves unemployed is a necessary feature of capitalism because of the competitive stress it places upon employed workers. Lawrence addresses this issue directly in talking about the importance of playing through injuries:

> Oh yeah ... if I didn't play, they'd call somebody up, which is always a chance that that guy takes your job. So if I was to say, "Oh, my groin's hurt a bit," right, they call Sean up and Sean plays great that night. All of a sudden Sean stays and I'm being sent to the minors. So I would always have to play hurt unless it was a broken bone or something.

Darin had a similar experience: "Well, for me it was because I was always on one-year contracts and I was a fourth-line player. So the more time you miss out of the line-up, the harder it is to get back in." For both men, playing hurt was an inherent function of the profession enforced by the industrial reserve army. The relation between all those unemployed players and injury confirms that subjecting the body to harm is a necessary part of the occupation for all but the most indispensable players. Whether or not management, other players, or fans explicitly demand that athletes play through injury, the competitive structure of the profession, with countless individuals aspiring to a precious few roster spots, forces players occupying those spots to guard them in any way they can. Allowing the body to recover from injury is simply not a risk they can afford to take.

Vasil makes a similar admission. After being asked about whether players are afraid to talk amongst themselves about their experiences with injury, he says:

> Yeah, yeah. I don't think that they're afraid to talk about it. Especially ex-players. I don't know about players playing right now. But players, after their careers, talk about it a lot more. They don't

like to talk about it during the season because I guess they don't want people to know and they gotta sign contracts and they got families, so that's why it's really confidential, but after the season they like to talk about it a lot more.

Active players are unable to speak with one another about their experiences with injury because of the fear that they will lose their jobs. They cannot afford to reveal any weaknesses because they have families they need to feed. It is only in retrospect that they are freed to speak up about what they have endured, at which point the concerns become a relatively ubiquitous topic of discussion.

If job insecurity is a common theme, the sense of being commodified is nearly a universal one. Lawrence makes this point particularly vividly when speaking of professional hockey players: "They're like wrestlers. They're like, you saw the movie *The Wrestler* with Mickey Rourke? … You're a piece of meat. You're a piece of meat, and once you're no good, you're no good." Lawrence is describing minor league professionals here, but his comments apply to athletic labour generally. The imagery of a "piece of meat" neatly serves as a metaphor for commodification for it shows the way in which the athlete, like a slaughtered animal, is reduced to an object that can be sold at market. The athlete's value as a commodity is tied to his ability to play. Once he loses this ability due to age or injury, he no longer has market value and is thus discarded. For the most elite players, sufficient compensation may have already been received at this point, but this does not hold for the vast majority in the professional and semi-professional ranks.

What Lawrence does not expand upon is the fact that the athlete *must* be treated as a "piece of meat" for the system to function. The athlete must be willing to treat his physical body as an object he is willing to destroy in order to fulfil his duty to the team. Yet, this is the body he is left with at the end of his career for the remainder of his life, even as the team simply moves on to a new, fresh piece of meat. This is the realization of Jean-Marie Brohm's warning about capitalist sport: "The specialists in this sporting Gulag stop at no human sacrifice in their drive to push back the limits of human capacity and transcend biological barriers."[1] Michael Robidoux says much the same: "Like a finely tuned engine, the player's body is driven to exhaustion, and, once the body expires, it becomes superfluous. Thus, the professional hockey player — more than any other labourer — is dependent on his body for productivity in his occupational domain."[2] The fact that some professional athletes are able to leave their careers with bodies they consider fully functional does little to mitigate the fact that all players have to risk those bodies during nearly every moment they perform athletic labour. It is in this sense that bodily sacrifice is a structural component of professional hockey.

Vasil talked at length about the way management treats players as commodities by pressuring them to play through injury:

> **Vasil:** *I have played through injuries. As a player, you feel pressure from the management above you ... I think a lot of players are afraid to admit it but there is pressure from management, you know, especially if it's not a bad, real bad injury, you feel pressure to play, especially the guys that are making a ton of money, right, they're expected to produce and play games and the reason why they're getting paid all that money is because they need them there and, yeah, the management might not say it to the media and be more vocal about it, but players know that they expect that from them.*
>
> **Nathan:** *Is that sort of an unspoken thing?*
>
> **Vasil:** *It is. Kind of an unwritten rule, kind of thing, I guess, but yeah, I guarantee you there's at least a hundred players in the* nhl *right now that are playing through injury.*
>
> **Nathan:** *Do you feel like there's pressure also from fellow teammates?*
>
> **Vasil:** *Yeah, yeah. Because, well, one, being a hockey player, you're noticed as a tough athlete and, usually with these small injuries, you kind of get picked on. Guys will pick on you, especially if you're out for a couple weeks and it drags on ... but yeah, players too, especially in big games and playoffs, they expect you to fight through it.*
>
> **Nathan:** *What about fans, did you feel any expectations from fans about playing through injury?*
>
> **Vasil:** *No, not really, no, they never ... fans are pretty much on your side always. They're pretty good, majority of them. I'm sure there are some that would say a few things, but majority of them know that speed and level and the commitment that these guys put into*

the sport with injuries that come, there's nothing that you can really do about it. Especially the real bad ones.

Nathan: *So would you say, in your own mind at the time, that playing through injuries was something you expected of yourself, or did you feel that it was the pressure from all these other outside sources that you've been telling me about?*

Vasil: *I think more about the outside, the management. I pushed myself through injuries too because I wanted to be there, and I wanted to play so I pushed myself to do it, but you're expected, like I said, you feel pressure, there's a lot of pressure from management and players and all that that people really don't talk about. But so I think it's more about that.*

Vasil's immediate response, unprompted, is to locate the pressure to play through injury with management. Like Lawrence, he suggests that it is widely understood that players are commodities who are expected to sacrifice their bodies in return for their wages. Additionally, implicitly, masculinity ("you kind of get picked on … guys will pick on you") and a sense of reciprocal obligation to one another also add to the pressure.

Sean identifies a similar phenomenon when asked if it was important to play through injuries:

Sean: *In the U.S. I did. I found, in the U.S., because you're so close to Canada, you know, you can … get another guy. You know, and again, depending on what the [injury] was, obviously, if I couldn't literally skate or I couldn't literally do something, but I never had an injury like that. But you know, high, sprained ankles and bad shoulders where you probably should take a week or two off to fix the problem. I wasn't good enough where I could afford to give up my position, you know what I mean? So any little thing, it was just show no weakness. They always used to say, "A long way from your heart." Guys used to take a puck in the ankle, and you'd get a badly bruised ankle, and they'd be like, "Yeah, a long way from your heart."*

Nathan: *Who would say that?*

Sean: *Your own teammates … Sometimes they'd be just joking around but you know, as a player … you didn't want to show* *that sign unless you were severely banged up. And the one thing I remember them saying, "If no one saw it." If you blocked a shot and no one saw it, you couldn't get away with it. You kind of had to play through the injury, you know, you have to. But if you blocked a shot hard and everyone kind of stood up and cheered and everyone saw it, it would kind of give you more cred. You know, a guy's slashed in the back of the leg, or whatever, right, if no one saw it, then it was kind of like, they'd question you why you're not at practice next, and not even games, practice. "Why weren't you at practice today? "Well, my, you know, I took a high-" Wouldn't happen. And that was from junior all the way up. So yeah, and those state of minds, it wasn't the best way to be, but you know, I'm glad, kind of, the game is changed a little bit where they take that a little bit more seriously, but at the same time, there [were] guys who were real good that milked stuff like that all the time and it would get to you as a player. Again, if you score fifty goals, you can get away with things like that. If you were just a guy, you know, moved the puck here and there really well and [laughs] play in your own zone, they didn't care. Those guys couldn't do that.*

This culture of masculinity is honed over years within a system that demands that players must play through pain for reasons stemming back to the economic structure of professional sport. Hockey culture itself becomes organized according to the model promoted by the business of sport. This has everything to do with economic considerations — political economy — at the professional level, for management requires players to give their all in order to make the game meaningful for fans, so that fans invest in ticket purchases, cable television packages, and team merchandise. At lower levels, this political economy exerts an indirect influence, for players and coaches emulate the behaviour they see at the higher ranks. Thus, although a culture of masculinity may appear to exist independent of commodification, its roots are embedded in the same ground. Yet, for Sean, the industrial reserve army is the starting point of any discussion about playing through injury. He notes that the culture of playing through pain is much more deeply entrenched in North America, where a large industrial reserve army exists, than in England, a place he spent much of his career, where it does not. He also makes it clear that the pressures of unemployed players are felt more strongly by those deemed dispensable than those considered to be stars.

Although players play through pain to prove their masculinity (which is separate from the direct influence of economic factors such as the reserve army), Vasil and James seem to have largely resisted adopting that internal pressure. Vasil retains the perspective that the pressure to play is externally imposed. This is relevant because it suggests that he, like James, Lawrence, and, perhaps, "at least a hundred players in the NHL right now that are playing through injury," experienced alienation as a fundamental part of his athletic labour. Even as these players played through injury, they remained aware that they were compelled to do so in the interests of others. As a consequence, they were alienated from their own bodies, which became instruments working on behalf of management rather than themselves. In athletic labour, the athlete functions as both labour-power and the means of production, for the commodity is the athlete's performance, produced through the use of his body. Unlike technology (a tool or machine), which is external to the worker, when the athlete's body wears out or malfunctions, it cannot simply be replaced — well, not for the worker. Because the labourer and means of production are one and the same, when management replaces the means of production/technology (the worker's body), they necessarily also replace the worker himself.

For all these reasons, the athlete is compelled to play through pain and injury. Indeed, to do so is normalized as part of the athlete's job requirements. Thus, for Luc, it was hardly noteworthy that he had to play through a broken jaw and concussion symptoms:

> Luc: *So that was the first time and it's, you just feel it right away and then my jaw was fractured at three different places. And, obviously, when you get a broken jaw, I mean, the chances are you are probably [concussed]. [Laughs]*
>
> Nathan: *And were you thinking about that even then?*
>
> Luc: *There was so much focus put on the broken jaw, nobody worried too much about concussion symptoms. So two weeks later, I was back on the ice, practicing and playing, wearing a big protector.*

Incredibly, two weeks after having his jaw broken and incurring a concussion, he was trotted back out onto the ice to play. This is what athletes are forced to put their bodies through. The fact that he laughed in describing it speaks to the banality of this event within hockey culture.

The most disturbing comments on this subject come from Curtis. He recounts how his body was consumed and then discarded in the business of professional hockey through a narrative of his experience with a grievous knee injury:

> Nathan: *So initially they made it seem like it was something that you would absolutely be able to overcome?*
>
> Curtis: *Yeah, oh yeah, absolutely. Initially, the injury happened in March and I was told I would be ready for training camp, which happens in September … So they just said, "You know what? We'll do the surgery, get some rehab going, you know, work out this summer, and you'll be back for training camp." They didn't make it out to be a big deal, so I didn't make it out to be a big deal. I showed up in September and still could not function and still couldn't move. Then they said, "Well, you know what, this type of injury really takes about nine months to recover." So you know, come Christmas time, then it became, "Well, you know what, this injury is really a year-long process." So they kept extending when I should be ready. So after a year, and I was still having issues with the knee, swelling and pain, then I started [to] become alarmed that something was not right and so then there was follow-up surgeries and everything else and it's a long story, if you've got time I'll give you the …*
>
> Nathan: *I do, absolutely. I'm interested.*
>
> Curtis: *[Laughs.] So basically, yeah, they did the surgery … I tore the* ACL, *the* MCL, *the* LCL *[ligaments], and the meniscus with the cartilage. So everything was torn, blown, everything. So they repaired the ligaments. They used what was called a "ligament augmentation device," a plastic ligament to replace the* ACL *that had torn. And, what is supposed to happen is that the scar tissue is supposed to surround the* LAD, *the ligament augmentation device. Eventually, that plastic dissolves and then the scar tissue becomes your new ligament, so basically, it's a process to rebuild the ligament in your knee … And that ligament, after a year, that* LAD *starts to dissolve on its own. And, what was happening was the scar tissue*

had not adhered to the ligament, so this plastic was floating around in my knee. Okay? But I wasn't told that, but they knew about it, because they did a scope on my knee a year after surgery. Actually, it was about a year and a half after surgery, because they kept saying I'm okay, just keep going, and I mean, I had massive swelling, I had pain, but they just said, "You know what? It's just a bad injury." That's what they were saying. Well, they did a scope on it and they did find that I had an exposed LAD. They didn't tell me. So they just told me to go back and keep rehabbing and keep going. The reason all this transpired was because ... there was a [work stoppage] ... So I was injured during the [work stoppage]. I was doing rehab ... I read in the newspaper, from [our general manager], there was a quote that said, "Curtis is healthy, we're going to clear him to play and his paycheques are going to stop at the end of the week." That was in the newspaper. And, this was ... Christmas-time. So they effectively cleared me to play during the [work stoppage] so that they would stop my paycheques. I come back from the [work stoppage], I can't play, but now they're screwed, now they can't say, "Well, no." [Laughs.] Now they force me to play. I go down to the minors, and this is where, you know, I'm trying to play and do all these things. I can't play, they're shooting it with cortisone, they're draining it, I'm not practicing. I'm only playing games every third day because I can't even walk in between. They call me back up to do another scope, they clear it out, this is where they're draining it and sucking all the plastic out. They make note in the doctor's notes that there's an exposed LAD which is a problem, because this LAD is dissolving, but it, the plastic just keeps floating around. So they're aware of the issue but they don't say anything to anybody. It doesn't come up until two and a half years later. So two and a half years after my knee injury, I go to see another doctor, a specialist in [another city], because now I can't even walk, I can't play. I effectively leave the team because now I know there's something seriously wrong. I go see [that city's NHL team] doctor, he wants to do a total knee reconstruction, tells me my career is over. I then get a second opinion from [doctor for a team in a different profession] and the first words out of his mouth are, "They screwed you, didn't they?" And I said, "What do you mean?" And he says, "They knew a year and a half ago that this surgery didn't work and they were covering up." I said, "How do you know?" He says, "Right here," and he points it out. And now, you and I could read medical notes and we wouldn't make heads or tails of them, it had to be explained to me what an exposed LAD *means. He says, "Right here in the medical notes, from that surgery, from that scope when they went in and checked it, they found the problem." And he said, "They knew back then." And I said, "Okay, well, now what?" He says, "Well, we've gotta take it out. We have to take it out, otherwise it's gonna keep irritating you. Yeah, but your career is over." And so this is how it all unfolded. It, you know, it really pissed me off, that, basically, I was treated as a piece of meat when they knew that I wasn't going to recover from this injury. They dropped me and, basically, you know, I was not given any assistance at that moment.*

Nathan: *That's so devastating to hear about. First of all, can you just expand a little bit more … about what was going through your mind? It must have been so difficult …*

Curtis: *I felt, initially I felt positive because I had a support team around me on the team, the doctors and trainers were supporting me and, you know, working through the process. And then, what happened over time was the trainers and doctors just, basically, left you alone to go and deal with it on your own. They didn't want to deal with you anymore, the team didn't want to deal with me anymore. You felt isolated and you didn't know where to turn. You didn't want to be that player that became the cancer in the room or upset the cart or anything like that, you try to go along with it as much as you can, but eventually, what happened was, I wasn't getting the answers I needed from [the team doctors]. They wanted me to keep playing through, they kept forcing me to go down into the minors on these rehab assignments. So these rehab assignments, they last two weeks. So every two weeks, they would reinstate me for another two weeks of rehab assignment and, after a while, even the doctors … on the farm team said, "You know what, you shouldn't be here. There's something going on." [He laughs.] They weren't aware. But they were the ones draining the knee and, shooting the cortisone. I was told cortisone should last three months, it should take the pain* *away for three months and, you know, grease the joint, and that should last. Cortisone, for me, lasted three days. Just enough to get through the next game and then as soon as the game is over, I'm on the table, I'm icing it, I'm not practicing the next day, they're draining fluid out of the knee and, after a while, eventually, you go, "You know what, this isn't right." But even back then, my agent was like, "You know what? Just play along, we're ... " because I'm in the last year of my contract, now. So there's a lot of outside factors that go into how you handle the situation. I'm sure if I had a long-term deal, you know, I could have handled it a little bit differently, but here I am, I'm trying to get a contract, I have to play along, and, but eventually, I think it was after the second or third scope I had [at the team medical facility], oh, what they would do is, after a month or so they would call me back up to go see the doctors, I'd get another scope, that's where they'd clean out the knee again, they'd suck all the plastics out and so on, and then they'd want to re-assign me back to the minors. And, on one of these occasions, I finally said, "No, I'm not going. There's something wrong. I know there's something wrong, but I can't prove it, I'm not a medical guy, I don't have the history with all the surgeries and everything, I just knew that there was something wrong." So that's, that's when I left the team and, I said, "I've gotta go see somebody else." And, I went home, and it was near the end of another season and it was just a long ordeal to finally get to the truth. When I finally got to the truth, I felt relieved that I finally had another doctor say, "Yes, this, I've seen this before, this is what they did to you." And, I said, "Absolutely, thank you, I'm not going crazy." That's basically how I felt at that moment, because it was a positive experience turned real negative and I was really pissed off at the end of everything, and finally there was relief, I finally had somebody understand what was going on and it wasn't just me, I actually had proof now of this.*

Curtis's experience screams out about the way in which athletes and their bodies are treated in the realm of professional sport. This is a kind and level of exploitation that is seldom appreciated by those who follow the games from the outside. Curtis feels he was treated like a "piece of meat" as well. The recurrence of this metaphor suggests that is has currency in the locker rooms of professional hockey. Curtis's story is an extreme study in what it means to be a piece of meat in professional hockey — an athletic labourer. The team and its management demonstrated no regard for his health or well-being as a person. Their only concern was for the production he could provide them on the ice. Likewise, there was no consideration of the long-term implications for his health, even with respect to his capacity to provide labour for the team. Given the wealth of replacement players available, management was not concerned by the possibility that they would overtax his body. Rather, their interest was in squeezing every bit of labour-power they could out of him before his body fully broke down.

This is precisely the advantage that wage-labour provides in capitalism: it is eminently disposable. The capitalist is always most interested in a flexible source of labour. Owing to hard-won gains made through players' unions, professional sport offers some lengthy contracts that can to an extent limit the rights of management over players' bodies. Thus, it is little wonder that management seeks to wring all the labour-power it can from a player while he remains under contract in order to provide a maximum return on investment. Curtis's experience, while extreme, is not exceptional. Curtis was unlucky that team doctors botched his surgery, for clearly it was in their interest to get it right. Once that occurred, however, it was entirely logical within the system for management to do everything it could to avoid paying him (during the work stoppage) and maximize the amount of production he provided them while still under contract. For those players privileged enough to be deemed indispensable by management (as represented by longer-term contracts), the pressure to perform through injury is lessened. For those who play in the minor leagues or at the edge of the NHL, injury is a constant struggle.

After his long narrative, I asked Curtis to reflect on what had happened:

> *[Long pause] I don't know, I mean, I don't know if I would have done anything differently, because we all did what we thought was best at the time … If I had to go through it again, I don't know that much would have changed, to be honest with you. Because, I think guys are still going through it today, I think it's the same thing. You can't rock the boat, you can't speak out if you don't have proof or evidence or something, or if you're being told something by*

the trainers and doctors, you just have to follow suit. You're not a human being, you're a number, you're a product, you're an asset as long as you can perform. If you can't perform, then you're a liability and they'll drop you.

It is painfully striking to hear someone who loved being a professional athlete — Curtis makes it clear elsewhere in our conversation that it was his dream and something that he loved dearly — speak about being completely dehumanized through the experience. *This* is the toll taken on most players by the productive processes of athletic labour. At the end of the day, the typical athlete, like other workers in a capitalist system, is "not a human being, you're a number, you're a product, you're an asset as long as you can perform."

Players endure injury because they feel that their very employment is at stake if they do not. In addition, the pressure to play through injury comes from the non-business, more social, side of professional sport in a couple of ways. First, professional hockey is a particular kind of social institution that encourages players to play through injuries because the sport markets itself as a site of toughness. Indeed, this is how hockey distinguishes itself from many other sports, like soccer for example. Hockey is the sport where players put themselves through anything. Fans come to the games because they identify with this toughness and sacrifice. This is what makes a game seem real and meaningful and important. Thus, the labour and stoicism of the athletes does social reproductive work for the fans by validating and legitimizing their investment in the game, even if players do not directly do it for this reason, but rather because of an employment imperative. Second, even the pressure that players place on one another is connected to this. Years of socialization within the system of high performance hockey have instilled the notion that toughness is an important badge of honour and part of being a good teammate. Yet, this ideology is predicated on an understanding on the part of management that players, especially top players, need to be on the ice in order to satisfy fans and also to demonstrate that playing is important enough that it will not be undermined by pain and discomfort alone.

FANS' EXPECTATIONS

As their comments show, players understand that their work, like all work in capitalism, is shaped by the system's dominant features: their bodies are treated as commodities from which all possible profit must be extracted, a process they are compelled to accept, regardless of pain and injury, because of the threat that they will be replaced. They do not perceive their labour to be significantly impacted by the demands and expectations of fans. However, this is not to say that fans do not enter into the picture at all. In fact, most players acknowledge the ubiquity of fans as part of their work as athletes. Indeed, much like retail workers who are confronted by consumers at their jobs every day, athletes encounter fans as an everyday element in their professional lives.

Lawrence sees fans as inextricably linked to his work:

> **Lawrence**: *You're always aware of them, because they're there when you're off the ice. When you warm up in the warm up, you see them in the stands. When the game starts, you know, you're concentrating on the game, but you're also seeing people in the stands. So they're always part of your life. The fans are part of the pro hockey life.*

> **Nathan**: *What did you think of them?*

> **Lawrence**: *Well, some you became, you know, pretty close with. There's fans where, they're fans of yours, so they talk to you after every game, and there's hecklers that you had no time for. So you had different people, different personalities that make it a lot of fun, or in a city like Toronto, if you're not doing well and you get booed everywhere you go, it's not fun to be there. So in my career, I never had any problems with any fans, except in [a city] when I got traded from [the Canadian city] back to [a U.S. city], I had a fight against, actually, a friend of mine and I got booed out of the arena and they said a bunch of bad things in the newspaper, just because, you know, the ex-teammate and, kind of, they felt I was a villain. But that was it, my whole career.*

In Lawrence's estimation, fans are by turns energizing and troublesome, but never irrelevant. They are part of the fabric of the "pro hockey life." His experience is echoed by Luc:

You know, at home, playing in [a traditional hockey market], obviously you're very aware of the fans... You know, different cities, one year I played in [the southern U.S.], so it was obviously not the same. Hockey was not even close to what it was in [traditional hockey markets]. In the mid-nineties, when I got traded [to a newer market], [it] was really at the stage where, you know, hockey was in development, you know what I mean?

Although the nature and magnitude of fandom varied in different cities, Luc makes it clear that the omnipresence of fans was a consistent part of being a professional athlete. Although this might be expected in the NHL, it is a factor even in less prestigious professional hockey contexts. Vasil experienced it in the AHL: "I think we were getting twelve to fifteen thousand fans a game ... So it was really, really popular for fans waiting for you guys outside for autographs and signing hockey cards. I also had hockey cards starting in the OHL, so you signed a lot of those too as well."

Although players were not specifically thinking about the desires of fans when they chose to play through injury, this does not mean that they were oblivious to the critical place of fandom in the business model of professional sport. In fact, most players were aware to at least some degree that the reason they had jobs as athletes was because fans were willing to pay to come watch them play. Chris, who played in the semi-professional OHL (out of which players are drafted into the NHL), was adamant that the significance of fans to the broader political economy of professional hockey was instilled in players from their earliest years playing the game:

Chris: *So it's all about the fans ... when you're young, your coaches tell you and you're like, "What? I'm just doing this for fun. I'm doing this because it's fun for me and my parents, I want to." ... They say, "No, you're playing for each and every fan in this ... " and you don't realize that, but then you sort of ...*

Nathan: *And your coaches are telling you that in the OHL?*

Chris: *They're telling you that in minor hockey [prior to the OHL].*

This lesson was not confined to Chris. Other players also had a similar understanding of the significance of fandom to their livelihoods. Vasil is particularly clear on this: "Without them watching your games, you don't have a hockey career. The excitement, the passion, right, it's tough to find people that are really passionate for teams and ones that are there day in, day out. But [where I played], there was, it was huge support like that." Luc also understood that interactions with fans were an inevitable part of the experience because of their place in the broader political economy of the game:

> Well, obviously fans are … if there's no fans, there's no profes-
> sional sports. It's that simple. I mean, you don't just play in front
> of cameras for TV, you play in big arenas with sometimes twenty
> thousand people there, so anyways, fans are very, very important
> and, you know, when you play as a professional athlete, you have
> to respect that in the first place. People are coming there to watch
> you play and perform and watch you, your team win, hopefully,
> and, so yeah, you have to know that and respect that. People are
> paying big prices to go see your performance.

He is acutely conscious of the connection between fandom and political economy, and of the implications of that connection: the fact that satisfying fans is fundamentally important. Although in other contexts Luc denies that the expectations of fans influenced the way he played or the decision to play through injury, his awareness of the significance of fans suggests that on one level he cannot to some extent avoid playing for them.

Outside of the NHL, in lower level leagues with more precarious economic structures, the significance of satisfying fans is even greater. This fact is not lost on players like Sean, who played in England:

> It was huge. After every home game, you'd have to go to the sup-
> porter's club. And, supporters that helped with meals on the road,
> and stuff like that, and they would do things, you know, for your
> apartment, or your flat in England. You needed a TV, they were
> always there to provide stuff for the team. So after games, there was
> always a lot of interaction with the supporters. So lots of times you
> would have a quick beer with them, and you'd do other things. So it
> was always huge to get the supporters on your side to make sure the
> gates would keep coming up, right, so it was a big part of interact-
> ing, and the school visits, and all the other stuff you'd have to do.

The obligations placed on players at this level extend well beyond their contributions on the ice. Players work off the ice to engender the investment from fans necessary to keep the whole operation afloat. If this means the players have to cultivate superficial relationships with the fans, then so be it. That becomes a part of their work as athletes. The players are expected to give spectators exactly what they need in order to stay interested. Chris speaks to a similar phenomenon in the OHL and elaborates on how this work varied depending on a player's status on the team:

> **Chris:** *Crowds bring in dollars and, just total revenue and the food and whatever, the beers. If the team's not performing, nobody's showing up, season tickets go down, no one's getting booze, popcorn and whatever, now there's trouble, kids are getting cut, they're bringing in new kids, trying to hope that something will happen. So the fans are the driving catalyst of it.*
>
> **Nathan:** *And as a player you're aware of that?*
>
> **Chris:** *Ye-, I mean, you are aware of that and you want to be, it's true, you want to be in the fans' good favour. So the worse you are, the nicer you are to the fans. That's what I will say. So the best players were the most disgusted in the fans. Because, number one, the fans are more all over them. And, then, the players who were just trying to get a good name and kind of fit in, are so nice to the fans and will talk to them and will chat with them after practice and stuff. The good players are like, "Aw," and then the good players will say, "Why that? What the f- are you talking to them for? What's the matter with you?" But they don't realize what it's like to have to schmooze your way in the, kind of, community, because they're just there on pure skills, pure talent and they're going places within a year or two. So everything is about the fans because everything's about the money, and the fans bring the money.*

There is little doubt that at the OHL level, players are vividly aware of the significance of fans to their jobs. Much like in England, this has implications for the way in which players must perform their labour. As Chris says, players with less job security feel it is incumbent upon them to do this additional work in the hopes that it will buttress their standing with the team. Whether or not this has an impact on their status, it is clear that the pressures of losing the job influence how players understand their own responsibilities to the team, including responsibilities to fans.

Despite the obvious significance of fans as consumers to the political economy of hockey, many players suggest they did not care what fans thought of them. Luc says he played for the team:

> Nathan: *Did you feel like you were having to play a role for fans, or did you feel like you were able to be yourself during your career?*
>
> Luc: *No, you don't try that. Personally, I never did that. I mean, you play the way you play. You play the way you're supposed to play under your team system and stuff like that … You know the fans are there, but … you play to win. And, if you win, you know that you make fans happy, but in other words, when you play, you play for your team, you play for your teammates. That's what it comes down to. You don't play for people watching, you know they're watching, and it's great. That's the approach I had. It's not like I was going on the ice to do a show, you know what I mean? I … was on the ice to perform, to do my best, and help my teammates, help my team to win, to achieve something. And if all goes well the fans and everybody else is happy. But I don't think you should go on the ice worried about playing for the people watching.*

Luc is explicit that his ultimate motivation is to play for his teammates, and he assumes that the indirect benefit of playing well will be satisfaction enough for fans.

If fans are part of an imagined community, players, conversely, live as members of a community that spend much of their time together. This community is deeply affected by the competitive dynamics of capitalism, but it is a community nonetheless. It is hardly a surprise that players esteem the opinions of members of this community over those of outsiders whom they perceive to be only contingent. This sense of externality is critical to the way in which players view fans and brings us nearer to an understanding of the dynamics of athletic labour as social reproduction.

Yet, for some players, being around fans is a genuine pleasure that validates their sense that playing professional hockey was the pinnacle of meaning and accomplishment. Darin fell very much into this camp: "Oh, I loved it. I mean, I was a fan too at one point, you know, I was a kid. So for me, I took every fan and every autograph very humble and very grateful." Curtis also received a tremendous amount of gratification from being acknowledged by fans, as he himself had once been a fan of professional hockey:

> I loved 'em. I loved the interaction, I thought it was a privilege to speak to them and deal with them and sign the autographs. Some people found them to be annoying, and I guess, at some points maybe they were, but for me, 99 percent of the time I was grateful and wanted to speak and interact with them and things like that, because, really, I was just breaking into the league myself, so I was still a fan [laughs], you know what I mean? I was playing with the people that I saw on TV and so when someone asked for my autograph, I was flattered and I wanted to make them feel that [I] was their friend rather than, you know, putting me on a pedestal. I had conversations with them or I spent time with them ... To give you an example, I had one fan in [Canada] ask me to attend his son's birthday party and so I threw on my jersey, hopped in the car and surprised the group. And I got just as big a kick out of it as the kids did [laughs]. So to me, I remember that, obviously, and I'm sure the child remembers that as a special moment, so I appreciated those moments.

Most players responded to the persistent presence of fans much less favourably, articulating a sense of discomfort, as if the interactions they felt compelled to have were somehow unnatural. Luc expresses it this way:

> You know, [fans] want [their team] to win, you follow in the news, on TV, and all that stuff. You care about the players. You want them to win and all that stuff. So as an athlete, you feel that ... just the atmosphere. When you show up in the big hockey cities, especially when you get down the stretch getting close to playoffs, and stuff like that, you see the energy change, the people at the practice rink, just there when players arrive, or before games, and things like that ... You know, the tough part, maybe that was one of your questions coming, the tough part is that it's very hard to develop good relationships with fans. I mean, they are so many, or it's like being idolized, so you pull up at the arena and there are fans there and

you know they want your autograph and it's a really, really special situation. I mean, people are there just to take a picture with you, to take your autographs, but it's not really a, you know, a personal relationship. It's really weird. It's something that, personally, I was never comfortable with as a player.

Luc speaks of fans in a favourable sense, distinctly aware of the fact that they care about players and hold them in high regard. Despite acknowledging the heightened "energy" they bring to the arena, he quickly changes tack. He shifts to what is difficult about the relation to fans, even assuming that this is the topic of a future question. He describes interactions with fans as "weird" and "never comfortable." Even his choice of the term "idolized" as a way of describing how he is perceived by fans — rather than, say "loved'" or "adored" — suggests artificiality. It is as if they are worshipping only a facsimile of himself, mere artifice in his image, a false idol even. He elaborates on his sense of strain in the relation to fans:

You don't know these people. And then these people don't really know you. All they really know is you as a hockey player, your number, and they've read stuff about you in different medias or heard stories on TV, or whatever, but they don't know you. You know, it's like, in the summertime, I live on the lake, and sometimes I had people just pulling on the boat in front of my house and filming, and taking pictures, so it's really, really weird. So it's tough when you're dealing with that, to develop relationships with people. I'm not saying all fans are like that ... There are fans that are really fanatics. In a bad way, yeah [laughs]

More than even most of the players I spoke with, Luc demonstrates a real awareness here of how fabricated the imagined community of fandom is and how much it relies on surveillance. What he seems to be getting at is the way in which players are dehumanized as an object on which the community affixes its investment. He is left with a "weird" feeling because this process is unnatural, even inhumane, in a way that is difficult for him to precisely pin down.

Chris too finds aspects of the dynamic between players and spectators disquieting when asked about his experience with fans off the ice:

So yeah, off the ice is a bit, it's more annoying. I mean, you'd have to come after the game and there'd be a table of things you'd have to sign, and you don't know these people. I mean, the kids, yeah, it's nice for the kids, but there are some, here's a booster club, right, who's supposed to boost the team, but I don't know there's some people who are like pedophiles, like registered sex offenders and stuff. I don't know, I thought some of them had mental problems. The teams would call, the team would call them "the critters." You know, it's the booster club, and they were supposed to be there for us, but we'd call them "the critters." And they would add you on Facebook and all this stuff and think that they were so involved in your life, like commenting and whatever. It's funny, I see guys that I know that actually did make the NHL, *the same critters ... are bombarding them with messages comments on Facebook, as if they know them. Like, "way to go, Damon," this guy who plays [in the* NHL*], Damon Daniels. And I see all these, and I'm like, "Oh my God, these fans are still at it." And, the thing is, they sort of latch on to the ones who make the* NHL*. So I'll see the few of them that will post on that guy's wall, "Congratulations to this guy, this guy, and this guy for their great seasons," and stuff. And I'm like, "Whoa, that's ... " I don't know. There has to be, there's something weird there. I mean, that's just my perception. You'd have a fan, some lady, you know, middle-aged or above middle-aged, lady who'd come to every single practice with her little dog and just sit there and watch. And sure, it gives a lot of people meaning, and that's fine, but as a player, they love you, and you're like, "Oh my God, ugh." You know, so that's the interesting part. But I mean, it's just fanfare. They're fanatics and it gets kind of weird when they're fanatics about you as an individual. The other side of the coin is that, when you're good, they love you, but when you're bad, it's in the newspaper, "What's he doing here? He should be on the bubble. He should be gone." You know? "Why's he? He can't score ... " So it comes with the territory, I guess.*

There is much going on in Chris's observations. On the surface, he is incredibly irritated by fans and the obligation players have to them. What makes this particularly interesting, though, is the way he characterizes the experience as artificial. Although fans "think they were so involved in your life," to him they were not. This meant that although his play was giving "a lot of people meaning," the process through which he did so nevertheless felt absurd. The reference to pedophilia and "mental problems" shows just how unnatural this dynamic seemed to him. (There is certainly an ableist dimension to the suggestion that mental illness is unnatural, but this appears to be his intended meaning.) Finally, he also demonstrates a consciousness that the fans had an impact on his livelihood. If they liked him, his life was easier. If not, it had the potential to drive him from a job. This love–hate relationship is entirely predicated on his performance; it is, in other words, the furthest thing from unconditional.

James shares Chris's unease with fans:

> **James**: *You don't really notice them on the ice. When [I was in the* AHL*], we were a pretty bad team so ... you're getting booed and stuff. But other than that, you don't really notice them.*
>
> **Nathan**: *What about off the ice?*
>
> **James**: *You've got fans that wait for you after the game, autographs, that type of thing, you have player appearances. I wasn't the biggest fan of the fans, but it was just kind of ... These people, they don't know you but they think they know you type of thing. They're all over you, especially social media and stuff, they can harass you a little bit, eh? Just tried to get into your life type of thing.*

His impression of fans accords with Chris's. There is a sense here that something is unnatural and forced about the relationship between players and fans, a feeling that they are insinuating themselves into aspects of his life in which they do not belong and have no right. When prompted, he elaborates about the expectations fans had: "You know, they would invite you for dinners and stuff, hang out with them, do this with them. And you were just like, 'It's not like we're friends.'" His reference to friendship underlines the fact that he understands the relationship between spectators and players to be superficial and artificial. It also suggests that he feels like fans perceive the dynamic quite differently than he did as a player.

The fact that some players find engagement with fans to be an unnatural and uncomfortable experience not only indicates the commercial exchange nature of the relationship between them, but it also shows something above and beyond typical work alienation. In other words, these gestures of unease open a window into the larger social process: players produce meaning through their play for fans while simultaneously playing for the profit of owners. Yet, beyond simply the production of profit, players repeatedly frame fandom as something superficial and external to their experience. They acknowledge that they must pander to fans — and in this gesture to a vague awareness of how the political economy of the sport is organized — but they generally suggest that they do not pay attention to fans (other than acknowledging that they receive a rush from the feeling of succeeding in front of a multitude, which I explore in a later chapter). In being compelled to acknowledge the presence of fans, they experience a form of alienation — their labour is not their own but is for someone else. Their very resistance to acknowledging that they care about what fans think or want — while simultaneously revealing an awareness of the significance of fans to the economics of the game — can be read as protesting too much. They insist that they are *not* playing for the fans, even as they do, precisely because they are trying to defend their sovereignty over their labour in the context of a capitalist system largely out of their control.

Athletes also experience commodification due to the tendency of fans to support teams rather than players. When asked whether fans cared more about the team than individual players, Darin remarks, "Oh yeah, for sure. Yeah. I mean, fans have their favourite players that they cheer for, but all and all, they want their team to win." Despite his feeling of connection to the fans, he is clear that they care more about the team than him personally. He knows that players are simply the vessels for the meaning of fans, to be readily discarded when a new and perhaps superior body is recruited to the task. Players are acutely aware of this instrumental approach that renders them replaceable. Luc reveals that he too has internalized the idea that the team *should* come before the player in the affections of fans:

It depends what market you are in. I remember, again, in a market [in the U.S. south], where people are really not knowledgeable about the sport, about hockey. I mean, people were big time fans of a [star player], and meanwhile the team is just an average team, you know? It seems like in some of the markets, especially in the States, where the mentality is like having your big star while people

are kind of developing their own stars. So anyway, that market in
[the U.S. south] was very much around the [stars] and meanwhile,
as a team, you didn't feel that it was like a fan [of the team], it was
more like a specific individual's fan. Which is not good, you know
what I mean? And that's a problem, very often, in some of those cit-
ies where they're not really big hockey cities. You'll play in Canada,
yes you'll have more highlights around certain players, but fans are
more knowledgeable and fans are a team fan and not, say, back
then, when I was playing, you know, you had the effect of, say, a
Wayne Gretzky going to L.A. or, you know, when Mario Lemieux
came to Pittsburgh. You know, people just got drawn to those teams
because now big all-stars were in those markets.

The most revealing aspect of this discussion of hockey fandom is the
way in which Luc has internalized the logic of the imagined community of
fandom. He is chagrined to find that many fans in markets where hockey
did not have a historical hold (markets where the imagined community
of fandom has not yet fully taken root) are more interested in particular
players rather than the team as an abstract entity. He is endorsing an
understanding of fandom that sees players as relatively anonymous and
interchangeable figures through whom the imagined community is given
life. This fact reveals the ideological power and scope of the imagined
community. Players are socialized to believe in its existence in their youth
and then come to reproduce its logic through their professional labour.
However, he notes that in particular contexts (such as his examples of
L.A. and Pittsburgh), the logic of making profits demands an initial focus
on a star player, rather than the team, before the imagined community
of fandom has fully formed. The star player helps build and consolidate
a market for the imagined community, paving the way for his ultimate
obsolescence once the community becomes fully entrenched.

Although Luc does not say so explicitly, there is an even more significant premise underlying his analysis: the business of hockey thrives when
fans are invested in teams rather than players. If fans are only interested
in watching particular stars, they will simply show up to the games when
those players are involved and neglect to purchase tickets or watch games
on television at other times. This leaves cities whose teams lack signature
players with little enticement to draw fans aside from the few occasions

on which stars come to town. If fans invest in the team above all, they have incentive to show up regardless of who is employed. Thus, it is in the rational economic interest of the team to promote enthusiasm for the abstract imagined community of fandom rather than individual players. It is the logical consequence of the economics of the sport — and the imagined community of fandom — that players are turned into replaceable human commodities.

Although the logic of the system dictates that fans support teams more ardently than individual athletes, this does not prevent them from turning against individual players when things go awry. The violence of this reversal suggests the level of meaning being produced. Because fans come to identify with the team, when the team loses, fans must displace their own sense of failure back on the player, symbolically expelling the player from the team. Consequently, players often experience vitriolic abuse at the hands of spectators. Sean witnessed an extreme instance of this phenomenon in England:

> *Theoren Fleury came over there, ex-NHLer, and he was playing against Coventry. Now, Coventry fans were very, very, very hostile and very crazy and they went at him pretty hard, like with his drug abuse, his alcoholism, and they didn't even cut back at all. And there was actually a picture, maybe you can find it, where Fleury was up over the glass and he was yelling at the crowd. Now, I wasn't there, but ... it was all over the, the media, the U.K. media, and I actually felt pretty bad for him, like here's a guy that's trying to move on with his life and that was being brought up.*

The more successful the athlete is at generating meaning for the fan — that is, the more impact a player has on the game — the more potential he creates for this abuse, for he makes the imagined community seem more concrete and real. This produces the potential for violent response, as the fan becomes inclined to displace the frustrations of life onto the enemy of the imagined community of fandom (who now appears to be a real enemy). The enemy, in an abstract sense, is the other team. Yet, the other team is embodied in the individual athletes, and it is they who bear the burden of this malice.

Darin experienced the wrath of opposing fans personally: "Just the normal stuff where you go to the penalty box, they're screaming at you, getting at you, and … maybe you'll say something back or you'll take a water bottle and spray them, but no fights or swinging or anything." It is notable how banal he finds being screamed at by fans — it is "normal." Players must endure this abuse as part of their jobs and it must impact them. Curtis makes a similar point after being asked whether fans care more about the team they cheer for or the players on the team: "That's a good question. I think it depends on how the team's performing. You know, if the team is performing well, they cheer for the team and they love everybody. If the team's performing poorly, I think they start to go after the individual." In general, winning and losing is an important part of the experience of the imagined community of fandom. Winning knits the community together; losing produces fissures. Some communities bond over the losing, others fragment. It is only logical that players would bear the brunt of losing, as they become targets for the displacement of the frustration of fans over the disintegration of the construct that gave them meaning and purpose.

There are many aspects of sacrifice that the athlete experiences that extend beyond simply being an athletic worker. One is injury and the crisis of identity that can follow. A second is the loss experienced as a consequence of serving as the vessel for meaning for fans. A third form of sacrifice is evident in the experiences of Sean, Darin, and Curtis: by generating meaning for fans, the athlete becomes a target of abuse. As the physical embodiment of the antagonist to the imagined community, he becomes an object of hatred and vitriol. This has the potential to be deeply destabilizing (for example, the experience of Theoren Fleury).

Another side to these dynamics is raised by Chris, likely because he is younger than the rest and the only one to grow up in the era of social media. He experienced the way that the zealotry of fans can manifest into obsessive analysis of young prospects who may one day become players in the NHL and vessels for the imagined community. That zeal evidently took a significant toll upon his psychological and emotional development:

> When I was young, for instance … I had even more success than I
> did in the OHL. I was in the newspaper when I was thirteen years
> old for being a top scorer and all that stuff. And it freaked me out
> to think that all these people that I don't know think they know me
> and are making comments about me, and I didn't understand that,

anyone can say anything, doesn't make it true. I would be thirteen and random people would be blogging about me on the internet, and I just was like, "You know what? I don't want to play hockey anymore. This is just weird." Even people I never met, under the anonymous, they'd be like, "Yeah, this effing whatever, you know." Just people are, the way people comment, especially with the internet, it's gotten worse. Everyone's a reporter, right? And, there's such anonymity ... And so everyone feels so strong and comfortable to say just crap, you know? So it's not, "Oh, okay, this article's by this guy with his face right there," and there's a bit of accountability there. Especially for young people, when you don't understand that. So that, honestly, I found it gets worse, and it's, you know, Twitter. I played when I was younger a lot with that kid on Montreal, Subban, I don't know if you know ... Scores the winning goal against Boston, and it's like, "Effing [lowers his voice, racial slur]," and all this stuff, "Oh this, that." And, I'm sure he has people who really can talk to him and say, "You don't worry about that." But when you're young, you're not worth any money yet, right, so there's no person that they're willing to pay to, kind of train, you know what I mean? It's that commodification again, it's, "Okay, well I've invested this many dollars in you, so if your head gets screwed up, then my whole investment goes in the garbage, so I'll pay this guy sixty grand a year to just basically coach you mentally in and out the whole team." But when you're young, and you have to deal with that, you don't get that. And, at the same time, like I said before, maybe the people who were stronger mentally when they were young are the ones who made it to the next level. Because, at the next level, the bombardment of media and social media is just, it's insane. So the scale just amplifies so that I think that no human can deal with that, because it's unnatural.

This is a harrowing experience. Even as youths, players become celebrities upon whom the attention — and ire — of fans and media is fixated. For Chris, there was a clear psychological consequence to this, as it caused him to question himself. At other points in the interview he spoke of nightmares that haunted him throughout his career playing hockey. It is no great psychoanalytic leap to suggest that these youthful experiences were scarring in terms of their contribution to his sense of self. His analysis here suggests that only those who are emotionally and intellectually calloused are able to advance through the gauntlet of elite youth hockey. These sorts of calluses must undoubtedly impact players after their careers end, for they are a sort of emotional barrier. In other words, by becoming the locus of meaning for so many people, athletes become compelled to isolate themselves from the social realm. Even as they reproduce others, they stunt themselves.

This real and imagined connection between players and fans affects both the way that players play and the decisions they make to play through pain and injury. While many players disavow that they are influenced by the expectations of fans, at other times players consciously acknowledge that they do play for fans. This is partly owing to the economics of pro hockey, but it is partly a reciprocal process between players and fans in which fans invest meaning in players and players mirror that meaning back to them, elevating themselves to the status of heroes and fans to membership in the team. Darin, for instance, explicitly acknowledges the impact the expectations of fans had on his performance as an enforcer:

> **Darin**: *They'd react to a hit or a cheap shot and they would go crazy, and then that would get me going. So it sort of worked hand-in-hand.*
>
> **Nathan**: *And did it matter to you a great deal what the fans thought of you?*
>
> **Darin**: *Well, I think not the away fans, but your own home fans, yeah, sure. You know, you want to be respected by them and liked by your home fans. But the away fans, I didn't really care about.*

For Darin, the way in which he performed was shaped by the reaction of fans, at least to the extent of fulfilling his responsibility to give "home fans" exactly what they were paying to see. Lawrence had a similar experience:

> **Nathan**: *You were telling me that there were different attitudes that fans have, 50 percent rock 'em, sock 'em, 50 percent want to go with their family. Do you feel like the expectations of fans ever influenced your own decision to play through injury? Or, to engage in behaviour that would make you more likely to get hurt?*

Lawrence: Well, yeah, because it becomes, you know, have you ever watched the movie Gladiator? … Okay, so it's like the Colosseum, and people are cheering for them, and when you're a player, and you're at home especially, they cheer, they're your life- line. You make a big hit, they cheer for you, you score a goal, they cheer for you, you get in a good fight, they cheer for you. So they influence you, they give you, you know, energy to say, "I want to be out there." They're a big part of why we play. Right? Twenty thousand people screaming for you gives you, you know, it's like this power, if you will.

The symbiotic relationship between fans and players is clear. The performance of the player rejuvenates the fan, who in turn redirects that "energy" back to the players in a feedback loop that serves to animate the imagined community of fandom. Vasil explains that even when players publicly state that they are impervious to the expectations of fans, this is seldom the reality:

Oh, for sure. Everybody's got pressure. Don't let players fool you. They try to play it off a little bit that they don't feel the pressure. But when fans and the media are on them, then they're definitely at home thinking about it. And, a lot of players say they don't, but in the back of their head they're thinking that they want to do well for those reasons too as well.

Players are aware of fans and what fans are thinking of them. The "pressure" Vasil describes appears to be a sense of responsibility to fulfil the expectations of fans, expectations that have to do with effort and investment as much as performance. Lawrence is similarly conscious of these expectations:

Lawrence: Oh yeah. Sure. Well, my role, and I, let's face it, as the fourth liner, they know when you step on the ice things are going to happen physically. So when we would get out there, and they would be cheering and screaming, and, in a sense, looking for blood, then, that was the way it was. It was different when Gretzky stepped on the ice.

Nathan: And you could actually hear them?

Lawrence: Oh yeah. When we'd line up against the other fourth

*line, you could hear the anticipation of who was going to fight.
Sure you do.*

What is noteworthy here is how conscious and aware he is of the fans and their expectations of him. He was fulfilling their requirements by performing his pugilistic role.

These experiences paint the expectations of fans in a somewhat favourable light, suggesting that they are to some extent energizing and motivating. Yet, this is not always the case. Sometimes players are unable to satisfy the expectations of fans — expectations they are acutely aware of — and this results in a significant sense of impotence and failure. Curtis describes this experience:

> *Prior to my knee injury ... it wasn't a factor what fans said, and mostly ... there wasn't a lot of negative awareness ... When you're on the road, you expect fans to boo and, you know, do all of those things, it doesn't matter, but this was my home crowd, in my home arena and just one particular fan who just would not let up, and you kind of wanted to look up at him and say, "Hey, you know what, I'm trying. I'm dealing with something you're not, you have no idea about." And that was the only time I felt frustrated. But I shared his frustration about how I was playing, because I couldn't play. I mean, he was right, I couldn't play, but it was, I guess, I wanted my hometown crowd to back me in support as opposed to, you know, giving me the thumbs down.*

Even more significantly, players tended to be highly aware of the expectations of fans about whether they should play through pain and injury. While this may not always have been as much of a factor in the decision to persevere through bodily harm as the need to stay a step ahead of the industrial reserve army and to remain in the good graces of teammates, it nevertheless seems inevitable that such a clear expectation must have informed the decision making of some players. Lawrence and Sean were two of many players to demonstrate that they were attuned to the requirements of fans on this subject:

> **Nathan:** *So one question that emerged out of what both you guys were saying is, you talked about how the air comes out of the arena*

when there's some kind of gruesome injury. Do you feel like fans bounce back? Do players bounce back more quickly or less quickly than fans when it comes to that?

Lawrence: *Well, I think the fans get over it quicker because ...*

Sean: *There's no connection to the players.*

Lawrence: *There's no connection. They're just drinking their beer or they're there as a game, okay, that's over with. No you got two other guys fighting here in the corner, it's a great stand-up fight and they're cheering again, whereas the player's are going, "who's the next to get hurt?"*

Here we have a clear and incisive statement of the difference between the way players and fans experience injury and violence. For fans, as the players are aware, it is a minor blip, quickly forgotten. For players, it is a crushing reminder of the dangers they experience every day in playing. It is also noteworthy to see just how conscious these players are of how expendable they are to fans. Lawrence goes on:

The Don Cherry[*] fans of the Rock 'em, Sock 'em blood bath, they go there, they drink their beer, they wanna see blood. They should be watching UFC [Ultimate Fighting Championship]. I take my family, my kids there, I don't want to see him lying on the ground shaking from a seizure with blood pouring out of his face. I want to see Crosby to Malkin, Malkin goal. You got 50 percent want to see hockey, 50 percent want to see blood. The percentages may have changed with all the violence, so maybe 65, 45, or maybe 70, 30. I don't know what the percentage would be today, but it's not pro-fighting so much anymore.

Players are acutely aware of what it is that fans want to see and that informs the decisions and behaviour of players. If a player knows a fan wants to see blood, he is more likely to provide it, whether it is his own or someone else's. Sean adds:

---

[*] Don Cherry is a former NHL head coach and long-time television analyst for CBC's *Hockey Night in Canada.* He is notorious for his advocacy of violence in hockey and his criticism of European players, who he claims play a less physical style than Canadians and Americans.

In a minor pro environment, I remember playing in Texas, and we had, like Lawrence was talking about before, about like booster fans that come down and talk to you. And usually, they would set up these little meetings after the game. You got up and you have a drink with the owners, the sponsors, the people that were putting in money towards it. And they, the question this one lady asked me was, "When does the referee tell you that it's okay to fight?" Or, "When do they cue you to fight?" So on that aspect of things, they just have no idea about, they don't even know if it's real. They don't even know if it is really a guy getting hurt, is it really somebody losing a job over this?

Again, we see here just how different the experience is for fans and players. Sean reveals that it was clear to him that fans had no conception of just how serious the stakes were for players. Although fans were entertained and found meaning in the games, they gave little or no thought to what players actually had to go through to make that possible. Vasil makes similar observations:

Vasil: *Well, I think that the thing with fans is that there's new players every year. Seven, ten, twelve new players every year, so they don't forget about the players, but also there's, within ten years, you're probably gonna go through hundreds of players. So they don't forget you, but that injury will always be in the back of everyone's minds in that organization and whoever was coaching, and the fans, but because he recovered from it, kind of, I think it was a little easier, but …*

Nathan: *So you feel like, if I understand you correctly, fans are more invested in the team than the players?*

Vasil: *Of course. Yeah, yeah. I think they're more about the team and team winning. It's small towns and it's a big thing. Same thing as the Olympics, you know. We're all cheering for Canada, so if you're from a small town, a professional hockey team, you're basically cheering on your team more than individual players.*

This demonstrates that players are fully conscious of the fact that most fans don't empathize with them personally, a realization no doubt born of years of experience of observing how quickly fans are able to move on from and forget about specific players and the sometimes traumatic experiences that they have.

Luc does not think fans understand the cumulative toll of the physical harm players experience over the course of an entire season:

> *Just referring towards the end of my career ... at one point I had a really, really bad cold and bronchitis and on top of it I was dealing with really bad lower back pain. So here it is, right, I have this back pain and on top of it I have a tough time breathing and performing at high intensity and when you play, like I was in a role where I had to play against the number one lines and centres of the other team, trying to do a good job defensively and, so it's really hard. And meanwhile, the fans, most of them don't know. So they're expecting you to be healthy, to be fine and all that stuff, but it's really the facts, especially at the end of the season.*

Although this might at first appear to be a somewhat mundane description of the aches and pains players go through, the issue here is that even when ostensibly healthy, players typically toil through all sorts of physical injuries. Yet, there is never an acknowledgment from fans of this reality. So players are faced with the double challenge of playing through the pain and attempting to play at the level they are capable of when healthy. Otherwise, they must face not only physical discomfort, but the displeasure of the fans. James makes a similar observation:

> *I mean, fans always expect the same thing, right? And a lot of the time, they won't know that you're hurt, because ... they expect you to play at the same level that you when you're not hurt, right, like, playing at a high level. And most of the time, they have no idea what's going ... If you're just bumped and bruised up a little bit, slight muscle pull, or whatever it may be, they'll have no idea.*

Curtis experienced the same thing in a more extreme form:

> *I'll give you an example. My career ended with a knee injury: I blew all the ligaments in the knee and, and I need a reconstruction ... And I was trying to, in my comeback, I was playing in the minors ... and there was a particular fan who didn't appreciate the way*

I was playing, but he didn't know that I had gone through, you know, really, it was about a year, year and a half of rehab and, and multiple knee surgeries and everything else, so their expectation was that if I'm on the ice, I should be able to perform as well as I had before, but I don't think they understand, I don't think most fans understand the physical demands, the physical beatings that players take that affects their play. People don't see that. They see the athlete, they see them on the field or on the ice, and they expect that performance to be there every night and sometimes the player is dealing with something, it could be emotional, but most times it's physical, that would limit them from performing at their best. And so players don't make excuses for it, because we all do our best every time that we're on the ice, but sometimes there are limitations that people don't know about.

This is the burden placed upon athletes that is unacknowledged by fans. It is a sacrifice that is not rewarded through remuneration (they are paid to play when healthy) or through esteem from spectators. It is what players *must* put themselves through — it is demanded by fans that they play — but the effects of doing so are largely ignored. Thus, even as players breathe meaning into the imagined community of fandom through their labour and willingness to sacrifice their bodies, they are aware that fans do not understand the genuine nature of the labour that is being done. They realize that fans do not know what they are putting their bodies through and the sacrifices that they are making for them.

The labour of athletes indirectly produces a particular type of product: meaning for fans. This process is alienating, but it is also absorbing and temporarily empowering for athletes. The crucial point is that the athlete produces something beyond entertainment as a commodity. He produces something that fans take away from the game, something that nourishes and revitalizes them. But how does the fan experience the imagined community of fandom and why do they desire to participate in it?

CHAPTER 3

MANUFACTURING FANS

Fans turn to sport to experience a sense of camaraderie and purpose that allows them to transcend the lack of deep purpose of their everyday lives in a twenty-first-century capitalist society, becoming for a few hours part of something larger than themselves. Whereas athletes view their work as fundamentally linked to the economics of pro sports, spectators tend to reject this notion. For fans, sport is a site of play and inherent meaning relatively unsullied by money and profit. This is not at all surprising: for the imagined community of fandom to have *real* meaning it cannot be a mere construct of big business.

INTERVIEWING FANS

The fans I talked with came to me through ads on online team message boards, Reddit, Twitter, and Facebook. These ads were shared many times, and I received interview offers from a number of people I did not personally know. The spectators I talked to included women, unlike the hockey players, but both the men and the women are predominantly white. This is representative of trends in hockey culture.

Tarik

Tarik is a twenty-five-year-old self-identified Arab man who came to Canada at the age of eighteen. He is single, lives in Toronto and is working in a professional management position. Tarik is the lone fan in the study who does not watch professional hockey. He is a fan of the Toronto Raptors and Toronto Blue Jays, although he recently became more of a baseball than a basketball fan. He subscribes to MLB.TV and previously subscribed to cable television for the sole purpose of watching sports teams. He is also a very frequent attendee of Blue Jays games, sharing one or more flex packs with some friends. He estimates that he spends fifteen hours a week watching games during the baseball season and an additional five hours reading about, analyzing, and discussing the teams he follows.

Thomas

Thomas is a twenty-two-year-old Canadian born man of English, Scottish, and German descent. He is single and attending university in Toronto. Thomas is a Toronto Maple Leafs fan, although he also follows the Detroit Red Wings. He primarily watches games at home, although he also occasionally watches at bars or at the homes of friends. Infrequently (due to cost constraints), he also attends games. The previous year he had been to two Maple Leafs games. He attends the Blue Jays and Argonauts more frequently. He devotes approximately six hours a week to his fandom, half of that spent on watching games and the other half on engaging in conversation and online discussion and interaction about sports.

Mason

Mason is a twenty-three-year-old Canadian-born man who identifies as white. He is single and works as an analyst for a social media company in southern Ontario. Mason says he is an "almost" obsessive fan of the Toronto Maple Leafs, although he also counts himself a partial fan of Anaheim and San Jose. He typically watches games at his home or those of his friends, although occasionally he watches in a bar for "big games." He seldom watches in person because of the expense, although he attends approximately two live games per season. He devotes fifteen to twenty hours per week on fan activities, with about half that time spent watching the games and the other half spent watching highlights or following the team in other ways.

William

William is a fifty-two-year-old Canadian-born man of English descent. He is married with two children and lives in Toronto where he works as a designer/illustrator. William calls himself a general sports fan, although hockey and soccer are at the top of his list. His favourite teams are the Montreal Canadiens and Manchester United. He usually watches games at home, although occasionally he watches them in a bar. He has been to a few live hockey games in his life in Maple Leaf Gardens in Toronto and Buffalo, but has never been to see the Canadiens play in Montreal. He spends up to thirty-five hour a week following sports. Much of that time is spent watching games, although he also spends considerable time on internet media and social networking.

Maria

Maria is a thirty-eight-year-old Canadian woman who loosely identifies with Italian ancestry. She is married with two children and lives in the Toronto area where she works in community recreation. Maria has "total loyalty" to the Toronto Maple Leafs. Although she is a fan and player of many sports, she considers hockey to be her favourite "by far." The primary venue for her spectatorship is her home, owing in part to the difficulty of getting tickets to live games. However, this has not stopped her from travelling to attend games in other cities, like Buffalo and Montreal. She also occasionally watches games in bars. In a typical week, she spends approximately twelve hours following the team, the majority of that time devoted to actually watching games.

Linda

Linda is a forty-four-year-old Canadian-born woman who identifies as white. She is married and works in the Toronto area as a lawyer. Linda sees herself as a hockey fan in general and a Leafs fan specifically, although she notes that this fandom is by "default" given where she lives. She also notes that she is a fan of Canadian Olympic and junior hockey. She primarily watches games at a local "hipster" bar or at home on her computer through a pirate site. She also notes that she would travel in Canada to attend World Junior hockey games in person. In a typical week she spends approximately five hours following her teams by watching games.

Paul

Paul is a sixty-five-year-old Canadian-born man of Scottish and English descent who identifies as a WASP. He is married with two children and lives in southern Ontario where he works in an advanced position in a religious organization. Paul is a general sports fan who is particularly interested in hockey, followed by baseball, football, and golf. His most prominent fandom is with the Toronto Maple Leafs, followed by the Toronto Blue

Jays. Primarily, he watches games at home, although he notes that he does not watch as many games as he once did. When his children were young, he was a frequent attendee of Blue Jays games because of the low cost. Cost generally prevents him from attending games. He is not enthusiastic about viewing games in bars. He spends approximately six hours a week following his teams, much of that time checking results and statistics on his mobile device. He notes that earlier in his life the amount of time spent was much greater.

Ashley

Ashley is a forty-eight-year-old U.S.-born woman who identifies as white. She is divorced and lives in southern Ontario, where she works as a legal assistant/legal clerk. Ashley is a fan of hockey, football, and basketball, with an emphasis on the first two. She watches many different sports and often enjoys watching games even when she does not have a pre-determined rooting interest, primarily viewing at home. She is a fan primarily of the AHL Hamilton Bulldogs and the NFL Baltimore Ravens. She also expresses particular enjoyment in watching games live and attends as frequently as she can through connections. She is a regular attendee of Bulldogs games because of the affordable prices. She spends approximately ten hours a week devoted to her fandom, much of that time is watching games, although some is devoted to reading about topics related to her sporting interests.

THE MEANING IN SPORT

With some exceptions and at times considerable nuance, the spectators in this study overwhelmingly reject the notion that athletic labour is connected to fan desire. Whereas athletes are well aware that they must endure injury to create the meaning fans seek, fans understand the game to be fundamentally about play. They feel like they are not complicit in a larger economic structure. Fans perceive sport to be natural, even inherent, not an institution they are responsible for sustaining through their interest. This fact is demonstrated in their reactions to athletic injury. Rather than identifying any personal sense of complicity in the harm done to athletes — in that these injuries would not occur if fans were not willing consumers of these games — fans tend to view professional sport as simply a timeless institution. Thomas elaborates:

As a fan of a team, I feel bad, but do I feel personally responsible? No. I'm not responsible for the injury myself, I'm not responsible for how that player acts on the ice, and I'm not responsible for his decisions, but I feel bad as a fan because part of me is like, "I don't want to root for you right now." But I still like the team and I still like the player. So it's more like a mixed feeling where if I had a Phil Kessel jersey and he went and slashed a player in the face and injured them for three weeks, probably wouldn't wear my Kessel jersey the next day [laughs] … I would still wear it, I wouldn't throw it away, I wouldn't go on the internet and be like, "I hate Phil Kessel," and stuff like that. But yeah, it would kind of upset me, but I don't take it personally … I don't sit there in my room at the end of the day when I'm trying to fall asleep and just ball over in my head how I'm responsible for that player's injury. I'm not that connected to the team.

Thomas is unequivocal in his rejection of the notion that fans have any responsibility for injuries to players, despite the fact that players would not be in a position to be hurt if fans did not attend athletic spectacles. This suggests that fans may have a less finely tuned understanding of the economics of the game than players, who are aware that their job comes down to putting fans in the seats. Fans, on the other hand, seem to feel as if they are watching a game that would be happening even if they (collectively speaking) weren't present. It is precisely this attitude that makes the imagined community of fandom possible. If fans viewed professional sport simply as an exchange relation, it would be difficult to affix much in the way of meaning to it. It is only by imagining sport as a realm that transcends economics that it can become the wellspring for fantasies of collective identification. Mason expresses a similar sentiment in not feeling guilt about player injuries:

I think the reasoning is, it's kind of like, they understood the risks going into it. Myself, playing hockey, I understood that things could happen, it's never anyone's real fault. There are the injuries that someone's being an idiot on the ice and will attack you in a certain way, but most of the time people are out there to win and do what they can for themselves. It's not "I'm going to take this other guy out." So knowing that they know the risks going into the game that injuries can happen and will happen, I wouldn't say I feel bad for the injury itself ... I do feel bad in the sense that it sucks that it happened. I'd like it if no one really got injured, but to me, it's just part of the game, so I don't feel too bad about it.

Mason demonstrates basic human empathy for the players, preferring for them not to be hurt. Yet, the idea that injuries are "just part of the game" prevails, reinforcing the notion that sport and the violence therein are natural and normal, thus absolving him and other fans of any responsibility for harm that is done to players. William makes a similar argument about injuries to players:

I feel for the family and the player. I don't feel guilt because they're doing something they are passionate about. It's their goal in life. I mean, I know how much work it is ... Knee injuries in football used to be career-ending, they still can be, although there's a lot more the doctors can do to rebuild knees and that sort of thing. You think about a college player who's that close to getting to professional football, which is their goal, their ambition in life, and, I feel sad for that player and the family ... We went through a situation a few months, you know, the beginning of the year, a friend of my son's ... he played hockey for the Michigan team ... Saginaw. He got cut from the team and that was his goal in life ... He committed suicide. So that's their ambition, to get to a stage where they realize that they're not going to be able to make, reach that goal, you know, if it's career-ending. So yeah, that's what I feel. I don't feel guilt because it's no different than any other job. I just feel upset for all their hard work, I know how much work it is. We spent hours with our kids and that was their goal, but you know at some point you realize, okay, well, this is fun ... And, when you get to that level, it's even more time, so I can't imagine you focus on that goal and then ... one day, someone literally takes your legs out from under you, then you know what they're going through and you understand. That's more what I feel rather than the guilt of enjoying a competition, because I know they're there for, that's their passion. It's not me driving them there, although I guess, if you ever looked at it in a roundabout way, it is the fans and that, but there's still passion there.

William refuses to acknowledge guilt (or responsibility) per se as a fan for what players endure. At the same time, he points to a devastating example of how traumatic the sports world can be (the suicide of a young man cut from a junior hockey team). He does suggest that the fans may be responsible for harm to players "in a roundabout way." On some level, he is aware of the insidiousness of the economy of sport, even as he evades a direct confrontation with that idea. And, of course, it is necessary for him to emphasize the "passion" of athletes over the ways in which they are exploited in order to sustain the meaning he and others receive from professional sport. Linda replies about whether she feels guilt about injuries:

> No. Absolutely not. [Laughs] No. These are people who, I mean, there's an assumed risk, and I think the level of assumed risk varies based on that person's individual investment, and here, players' individual investment is high. This is their job. In the higher leagues they get paid well, I mean, in the NHL they get paid extremely well to do their job. With the understanding, this implied consent to some physicality that is likely to result in injury. So no, I think they've assumed that risk. There's times where they don't, and I will feel bad for them. And I'll go back to the Bertuzzi-Moore hit — nobody, nobody assumed that risk. That was not, it wasn't considered an appropriate part of the game, and it wasn't something he was asking for and it wasn't knee-on-knee incidental contact, it wasn't a check gone wrong. But I still don't even feel responsible in those situations because, you know, just like nobody feels responsible about what happens in my day-to-day professional career. There are certain risks that we assume.

Linda's is perhaps the most vehement denial, as she completely dismisses the notion that fans might have any responsibility. Indeed, her laughter suggests that she considers the very question to be absurd. In making an analogy to her own work, she suggests that the level of responsibility that fans have to athletes is equivalent to that any random person has to any other for what happens at their jobs. This equivalency elides the social relation that exists between athletes and spectators as producers and consumers of sport. And it does so because fans *must* misconstrue this relationship in order to derive satisfaction from professional sport.

Refusing to see themselves as complicit in athletic injury is not universal among fans. Some people are able to watch and draw meaning from sport without losing perspective on the political economy that fuels it. Paul is such a spectator:

> *If the hype to win is such that they feel the responsibility to get out there even although their instincts tell them that they are actually, could be, putting themselves and their long-term life in jeopardy. Why take steroids and, and all of that, I do feel a measure of responsibility. Because, I don't think anybody does things which are detrimental to their body, unless, well, it's self-serving in the sense that they want to do well and make as much money, and get the pride of winning, but there's also a lot of weight of responsibility of the fans to, "Get out there, you bum." And so I think ... I do feel some measure of responsibility. And, I respected, I don't know if I'm a big Sidney Crosby fan, I don't think I am, but I admire him a lot and I must say that I think that the way he conducted himself with his head injuries was impressive for a young man ... Now, he already had succeeded immeasurably, but I mean, to have a life ahead where everything's in the past is tough for a guy, so I think he wants to keep playing and I think he will and is, but I've been impressed in the way he has insisted on the best care and he's had a right to. He's also challenged the sport on it and, in short, I do feel a measure of responsibility and, when teams encourage athletes to do what's unhealthy for them, ultimately they're doing it because they think it's good for business, i.e., the fans want them to do it.*

Paul demonstrates a real consciousness of the business of hockey and a sense of responsibility for what happens to players. Maria also picks Sidney Crosby as example of athletic injury. She is clear that players like Crosby are exhorted to play through injuries such as concussions because of the economic implications of their presence on the ice:

> *And, who was it, Crosby coming back too early with his concussion didn't do well for him. So I think you kind of behind the scenes have this battle going on with coaches and managers and people who are invested with money want players back, with fans to get them, but doctors are kind of saying, "Hmmm, not quite." And so you've got this battle going on with players stuck in the middle and it's*

come back, don't come back. And some careers have ended, some have not, you know?

Maria is attuned to the fact that fans want players to play through injury for the benefit of their team, even when it is not in the player's best interest to do so, and the league wants to make fans happy so that they will continue to contribute to their revenue. But on the question of responsibility of fans, she shows some ambivalence:

Good question. I don't know if it is so much a responsibility person-ally, but more of a, I don't even know if responsibility is the right word that I want to use, but more like as a fandom, if we didn't want fighting, if we didn't want body checking, or we could better handle this situation, then it wouldn't have happened. And other times, responsibility isn't even with the fandom wanting something, like, you've got Don Cherry's Rock 'em, Sock 'em hockey, God knows what number now, and fans want that, they eat it up. But also when you look at a replay and you see what a player has done. You know, because sometimes they'll turn themselves just to get a penalty drawn for the other team, but they don't realize that if they turn, they now really put themselves in danger, and you get upset with them, but then is that part of what the rule change, is it a direct result of the rule change? Do we need automatic icing, is there a penalty, it's so funny now with the NHL right now and with their rule changes and what Bettman's implemented since he's gotten in and I'm not a fan of his. I'll be glad the day he's gone because I think he ruined hockey. You know, it's not what it was, but I'm not meaning in the sense of the fighting ... I think it's all part of the bigger picture, it's not necessarily us. It's managers, it's coaches saying, "Get out there and hurt someone." Because, you don't know where that injury started in the sense of, did the coach say, "I want you to hit him." So in that sense I don't feel responsible, but I feel respons-, and, again, I'm not sure if "responsible" is the right word. I feel bad for the mentality of the sport and the way it's been fostered and been allowed to develop to that point.

Maria understands that fans are complicit in athletic injury due to the political economy of the sport. Nevertheless, she pulls back from stating this definitively and unequivocally. She struggles with the word "responsible," as if she knows it is applicable and yet cannot bring herself to use it. Indeed, she ends up delivering an extended meditation on the culture of the sport and her antipathy towards its commissioner as a way of circumventing the question of spectatorial culpability. Maria comprehends the fundamental tension faced by fans, even those who are sensitive to the costs of violence in sport. While she is aware that some fans crave this violence and subsidize it through the money they funnel into the game — and feels uncomfortable with that — she is unable to fully acknowledge this reality by naming it as the "responsibility" of fans. To do so would undermine the precarious foundation upon which sports fandom is constructed: the idea that the game is inherently meaningful.

The next question we are faced with is just how much meaning do fans ascribe to professional sport? Sports fandom takes the form of imagined communities, abstract collectives in which fans come to see other fans as members of a large network of people who share a common bond through their investment in and support of a professional sports team. What does that investment and support look like? Benedict Anderson wrote that members of a nation were "willing to die" for the abstract entity they came to identify themselves with. It is little surprise, then, to see the intense level of enthusiasm fans feel for their teams. This enthusiasm is completely out of proportion with any notion that they are simply enjoying a commodity or spectacle, and this accounts for their rejection of complicity in an (exploitative) economic structure. No, they experience sports fandom as relatively unmediated and unmitigated meaning.

Tarik's love of the Toronto Raptors provided inspiration for a move to Toronto in the first place: "Raptors was one of the main reasons, well, not one of the main reasons, but a very strong reason why I moved to Toronto. I was very into [the] team and I had an opportunity here and, I was like, 'Oh, yeah I get to go and see Raptors games now.'" Although the move was not exclusively about the team, it allowed him to justify the decision to himself:

> So I eventually moved to this city ... A love interest brought me over here but one of the reasons why I was able to justify it ... was the Toronto Raptors. I was very excited about that. I believe the first

time I came to the city to visit it was a Toronto Raptors game and I fell in love with the city ... and the team.

Thomas elaborates on the type of affection he feels for his favourite teams by discussing what it would be like if one of those teams moved to another city:

So if I was a Montreal Expos fan, and say I'm a Toronto Blue Jays fan and the franchise folds and they move away, I'd be devastated, I'd be really depressed. And, I think, reading critics or sports journalists or general comments online about the Expos can really support that claim that, you know, a city would be devastated losing something as iconic as their baseball team and I would be in that group of people being devastated. Very much like if you want to bring that word "love" back into it, it's a very subjective word, but ... say you love your girlfriend and she leaves you for another city, or for another partner or whatever, you'd be devastated, and I think it would be similar. I don't know if it would be as much, but it would be similar. Yeah.

This is a very strong and thoughtful assertion. Although saying that one "loves" one's team is something that many would do in passing, Tarik has taken the care to flesh out exactly what that means by equating it to the love he might have for a partner. There are material implications to this passion. In order to sustain his interest in the team, he has had to make a significant outlay: "I used to have cable for the sole purpose of watching the Raptors and that was something I had in university and something I brought with me when I was here, but I eventually cancelled that in favour of going to more live games and Blue Jays games and there was kind of like an opportunity cost there, obviously." He adds later that he has an expensive television for the sole purpose of watching sports. For Tarik, "the Blue Jays are, not the centrepiece, but are definitely one of the jewels in the crown of my love for the city. So them leaving definitely would have an impact on my fandom, would definitely have an impact on my social life, would definitely have an impact on my overall happiness, obviously, that's negative." Maria echoes this point, suggesting she too would weigh her fandom into a decision about where to live: "I think it would affect me that I wouldn't even move out of the city, or if I was to move, I would see if they have access to, you know?"

Thomas describes his passion for the Toronto Maple Leafs in different terms:

I'm a passionate Leafs fan, but I try not to get too emotionally involved in terms of, how some people get really physically upset and put extreme rants and stuff on the internet or like getting into bar fights and stuff. I like to see them win, I don't really like to see them lose, but I don't get too upset about it. But I do have a passion. I follow individual players, I take into account when they make line changes, when the coaches make trades, stuff like that. So I mean, I'm passionate but I try not to get too upset or too angry about things in sports, I guess, if that makes sense.

Thomas assumes that the typical sports fan is "too emotionally involved" to the extent of "extreme rants and stuff on the internet or ... bar fights and stuff." Although he doesn't identify with these particular behaviours, he nevertheless sees himself as "passionate" and identifies these characteristics with "some people" — evidently these are other fans he has observed. This does not mean he does not feel a significant degree of investment himself:

It's gonna sound kind of cheesy, but when your team does well, you kind of feel like you do well. I don't really carry that over into every aspect of my life, where if the Leafs are doing well, everything in my life is going great, but I feel like, if I go to a Leaf game, because I'm invested in the team, and I like to see them win, when they win I feel like I'm a winner. And, that may be kind of weird, it may be kind of sad, in a sense, that that's how you equate happiness in your life, but I don't know, that's what I get out of it. I feel happiness when they win. And, I don't really know where that comes from ... I just, I feel good when my team does well. I feel good when my favourite player scores. And I feel bad when a player I don't like scores against my favourite team ... You feel like you're invested in the team, like the team is almost a part of you.

This is a clear and succinct a statement of the meaning of fandom. Thomas is filled with gratification and meaning through his investment in the team. It makes him feel like part of something larger and more successful than himself and this makes him feel better about his life. Tarik talks about what it would mean to him if he were deprived of access to his favourite team:

> *Um, yeah, I could do that. It wouldn't be the same. But if, in some weird circumstance, I'm not allowed to watch Leaf games, I could probably see myself following another team just to kind of fill that void. It would not be as intense ... because having a team to root for when you watch sports makes things more interesting ... That's why I'm into hockey more than, say, football, because I don't pay attention to any specific teams, especially for the NFL [National Football League], so I don't feel that invested in it.*

Thomas characterizes not having a team to root for as producing a "void" that would need to be filled in his life. This imagery, deliberately or not, connotes how large a place inside himself is filled by sports fandom. He says it would "not be as intense" to follow sports without a rooting interest, which confirms the intensity of his current experience and also suggests that he sees it as something more than just an arbitrary affiliation. Like Thomas, Mason identifies as a fervent fan of the Toronto Maple Leafs:

> *So my go-to hockey team is Toronto Maple Leafs. Again, born and raised into it living in a suburb of Toronto. Honestly, it's funny, because over the last, probably five to ten years, it's gone from, you know, just watching and not thinking too much about it to almost an obsession, it's really kind of bad at times. But because the team struggles now and then, thinking, "Okay, maybe I'll not watch hockey or not watch it as much." But I just have to watch it. I have to keep cheering for them, can't really switch teams.*

Mason's fandom has actually accelerated in "the last ... five to ten years," when he became an adult, inheriting more of the burdens faced by adult working people. Also note that his "obsession" with the Leafs is something of a compulsion, which speaks to the seemingly inherent nature of the imagined community of fandom: fans feel that their fandom is innate. Yet again, it is possible that it is the desperation of the need produced by capitalism that is actually responsible for the depth and strength of the craving for the imagined community of fandom. Indeed, Mason acknowledges that the allure of fandom is being a part of a community:

> *The passion that I feel when the Leafs win, or if getting into the playoffs, and stuff like that, being part of that community, that pride of your team, that's something I've never experienced before. And, I think that a lot of that comes from being part of a hockey team myself since I was five years old. Having that, the closeness with those guys, throw their bodies in front of a flying puck just to help you out or having the teammates that will do anything for you, and understanding that passion for the game and knowing that these guys go out there day and night with that same passion to try and win for the city is something that I truly respect. So then, knowing they're fighting for that, being able to cheer them on, whether it helps them or not, but [laughs] I'd like to think that it does, when people are in the crowd, screaming at them, being part of that audience that truly loves them is just an amazing feeling.*

Mason equates his feelings as a fan to those he has as a member of a team; it is belonging that he seems to seek. What is most interesting is that he considers the "passion" he feels for the Leafs to be "something I've never experienced before." Something has been missing from his life that feels satisfying and necessary. The Leafs play such a pivotal role in his life that, when asked if there is any circumstance under which he could ever imagine giving them up or switching allegiance, he, like Maria, considers this possibility unfathomable:

> *I honestly don't think I could ever do that. I don't really have logic behind it, I just, because I have grown up being a fan, switching teams just seems impossible for me because I would always try and find a way to figure out how the Leafs did, or even if I had no contact with them but I knew they were there, I wouldn't be able to, I wouldn't be able to cheer against them. [Laughs]*

His pleasure, it seems, does not come simply from cheering for *a* team; it comes from supporting *his* team.

William is considerably older than Tarik, Thomas, and Mason, yet he shares a similar devotion to his team. He explains why community built around professional sport is actually more profound than that organized around the nation, for example:

> **William:** *Club matches, if you go wearing your colours into someone else's club, you might have a problem ... I think the World Cup is a little different, because ... they're passionate, you know, it's national pride, if you're Brazilian or Italian, but it seems to be a little more, because I wouldn't mind to actually go to a country where the World Cup's being held. Not necessarily to go to the games, because they're really expensive, but to, say, in Rio, in the next couple weeks, to be on Copa Cabana beach where they have the big screens. A buddy of mine has gone a few times and he said ... you mingle with people from all over the world, and they're wearing their colours, and ... there's that pride, but there's not that [claps] clash that you get with the club games ... You know, when you go into Turkey and if you're a Man. United fan, you may not come out without [laughs] being in a scuffle of some sort ... It's a different type of passion with the World Cup and that type of thing ... They don't see the national team as often and there's an attachment, it's more national pride. Obviously, when it gets down to the nitty-gritty, you know, the final game, if it's the Italians and the Germans, or ... if it was England-Scotland, there might be a little more, you know, because there's political background there [laughs]. So there might be a little more that way. But if it's England-Brazil, it's not quite ... I think it's because the club soccer, you're watching them day-in, day-out. You're watching them every week and every year and you have that deeper attachment to your club.*

> **Nathan:** *And, do you feel any similarities with hockey clubs in terms of the dynamics you are talking about?*

> **William:** *Oh yeah, yeah. I don't have that hate, but there are a lot of people that do. You know, my sister-in-law despises the Bruins, despises anyone that's associated ...*

> **Nathan:** *And is she a Habs fan?*

> **William:** *She's a Habs fan. Yeah. She's born and raised in Montreal. So you know, I don't have that hatred. I do if someone's nasty to me. Then I dig in. But I have to be provoked into it ... If I go to Boston*

and sit in a Bruins bar as a Habs fan, I may not wear my colours,
but it would be fascinating to talk to them, you know.

William suggests that emotional attachment is actually deeper when it comes to the club side, which seems counterintuitive given that the nation is the original imagined community. The constant performance of rituals and the visceral pleasure of competition at the heart of the imagined community of fandom seem to provide a more concentrated form of much of what the nation offers. The imagined community of the professional team provides the normality and stability of daily or weekly play during much of the year and has come to offer plenty of opportunities in the off-season as well. The advent of electronic media has made the free agency periods of the off-season a frenzy of excitement and uncertainty that captivates fans nearly as much as the games themselves. This constant immersion in professional sport serves to concretize it as something real. The very fact of its banality produces an illusion of timelessness and permanence. It is always here, therefore it must always have been here. This produces a profound sense of identity, one that leads to an us-against-them lens for the world. Fans come to hate the other team's fans (Bruins fan, in this example), because they represent what the community is aligned against. Because there is so little tangible substance to the imagined community of fandom — it is based on little more than dressing in common signifiers and cheering on a team of employees — the other against whom the community is defined becomes all the more important. If fans do not know exactly who they are, what they do know is who they are not: a Bruins fan, in this case. William elaborates on the nature of the meaning he draws from his fandom:

> *I remember my mum saying before I got married, "You're never going to find someone who loves sports as much as you, you know, you gotta slow down because you're never going to find anyone and you're going to ruin any relationship you're in because you watch too much sports." … So when the World Cup starts, obviously, business, I work from home, business comes first [sighs], so I might have it on in the background, and if it's a game I want to watch, I'll tape it and watch it later, so I'll do that too. If I'm away at the cottage, I'll tape it, but I may, I'll take the laptop up to the cottage [laughs] and see if I can …*

Sport becomes a primary emotional source in the life of the fan. In a sense, it functions as social reproductive work contracted outside the home (even if consumed within it). Fulfillment is found through the vicarious experience of watching games and connecting impersonally with fans over social media rather than through interactions with family or even friends (who, as we have heard, are for the most part not fans). William further explains when responding to the question of whether personal difficulties influence his spectatorial tendencies:

> *I might watch just to kind of take my mind off things. I may not be as excited and that. Although, in a sort of reversed way, my family … claim, and it's probably true to some extent, that I'm miserable if [Manchester United] lose. So you know, if, sometimes mid-week they have a Champions League game and I'll be watching and if they come home later and I'm kind of quiet, and that, "What, United lose?" [Laughs.] And I say, "Is it that obvious?" So yeah, in a sort of reverse way, it does … Yeah, it does affect me. I'm sure it does. Ask my family [laughs].*

This is an interesting moment. It appears at first that William is going to say that sport is a form of spectacle (he "might watch just to kind of take my mind off things"). However, his line of thinking quickly turns in a quite different direction. Instead, he reveals that his fandom influences his other social relations. This is a compelling moment in terms of the power of fandom as a substitute for social relations. His emotions, he says, are *primarily* influenced by sport, not by interactions with loved ones and, indeed, he finds it largely impossible to prevent the ebbs and flows of his emotions about the game from affecting those other relations. This confirms that sport reproduces a particular type of experience of the world, namely one that is alienated. Although investment in the team temporarily fills the void caused by the individualizing nature of capitalism, it also actively prevents that void from being filled more organically (or in ways that challenge the dominant system) by other forms of social relations. This means that it is difficult for William to miss even one significant game:

> **Nathan**: *Did you ever feel a tug if you were missing a Habs game because you were at your son's game?*
>
> **William**: *It depends on what the game was. If it was the playoffs,*

although, they don't necessarily overlap as much, but yeah, yeah. I've felt that way with the United games as well. But not to the point where I'd be miserable or upset. I'd tape it and watch it later. I'd skim through it and if it's not going well, I'd just shut it off. [Laughs.] That's very convenient. "Oh, I don't need to waste two hours on that. Yeah, they're gonna lose." And, if they came back and won, I'd go over it again and see how they did it [laughs].

This is a strong statement of devotion to the team rather than simply sport more broadly. If William was simply a fan of sport itself, his enthusiasm would likely be satiated by watching his children play — this is, after all, a more directly vicarious form of fandom. Yet, he cannot help acknowledging that even as he watched his own children compete, he still felt pangs of regret not to be watching his primary club team. This was true, despite the fact that he *was recording the game to watch later* — he was not going to miss it. He goes on:

I watch as much as I can, but I don't think I'd miss it … I've been away for a couple weeks and not watched anything, but when I was down in Costa Rica … Oh, that's not true, that's not true. The Habs were playing and I was sitting, it was perfect, it was perfect, because, your afternoon siesta, so at about four or five o'clock, the Habs game came on, and they were playing Tampa.

Although William wishes to articulate a more disposable relationship with his team — he could replace, or at least supplement, it if he had to — when he actually attempts to make this case through an anecdote about a beach vacation, it turns out that he could not actually tear himself away and watched the games during siesta time while his wife slept. Again, his fandom intrudes upon his personal social relations. He continues:

We were into our room at about five o'clock after a day on the beach or the pool, or whatever we did, and so my wife likes a little siesta nap and I would just kind of turn the computer on, hook up, and watch the game, and then we'd go out for dinner. So yeah, I guess I'm a bit of a fan. But I feel I could, kind of, drop it if I was given, sort of an ultimatum, or was cut off or whatever, I think I, I could live without it. You know, there's other competitions [laughs].

Even as William asserts that he could step away from sport if absolutely necessary, he cannot help but provide the final, subversive rejoinder: "You know, there's other competitions."

Maria is perhaps the most passionate of all. When asked how strongly she feels about the Toronto Maple Leafs, she responds: "Oh, oh, total loyalty. Doesn't matter, win, lose. I started watching way back when with the Harold Ballard and they pretty much sucked, but been with them for a very long time and won't change. [Laughs.]" Given the strength of her allegiance, it is little wonder that her rituals for watching games involve total concentration:

> Nathan: *Can you just describe, when you're watching at home, the typical experience of watching a game?*
>
> Maria: *You really want to know what I'm doing? I'm swearing at the* TV! *[Laughs] I'm totally swearing at the* TV *if my kids are not around, if they're in bed. I will* PVR *[record] from the beginning and watch from the beginning, I don't want to know the score. I don't know. Yeah, just yelling a lot at the* TV, *watching it, talking with my husband about it.*
>
> Nathan: *Yeah, so when you're watching, it's not like it's in the background, you're watching the game?*
>
> Maria: *It will not be in the background. It's never in the background for me, no.*

Watching a game is total engagement and interaction. Maria's passion leads her to communicate with the screen, as if it could be a conduit to the players themselves. It is clear that fandom is more than simply a hobby in her life:

> Nathan: *Okay, so how important would you say being a fan of the Leafs is compared to other leisure activities or hobbies you might have?*
>
> Maria: *It's definitely more. I'm not even sure how to answer that. I don't know if you can put into words ... [long silence while thinking] It's, it's, I don't know. That's a crazy question to ask, I've never thought about. I don't know. Maybe we can come back to that question? I'm totally not even sure how to answer that because it's*

been so much a part of me for so long that you, I almost don't give it a second thought. It's like breathing, it just happens. It's, the Leafs are, yeah, I have no idea, that's crazy! [Laughs]

Maria's complete inability to articulate what distinguishes her fandom from other hobbies speaks volumes. She sees it as a natural part of herself and her life. This is a crucial element of the imagined community that cannot be overstated: it takes on a life of its own as something real and essential, a fundamental part of a person's identity. There are no circumstances under which she can imagine giving up hockey fandom from her life, including even new information about injuries: "Stop me from watching hockey? No, I don't think so. If you can stop a guy from getting a concussion, then I'm all for it ... It wouldn't stop me from watching it. I don't think anything really would stop me from watching hockey."

Eduardo Galeano remarks that sport is the only religion without atheists.[1] This is worth keeping in mind when considering the sentiments of Paul when I ask how strongly he feels about the Leafs:

Well, you know, you joke about it, but I would be lying if I didn't say that sometimes emotionally it does impact [laughs]. I, jokingly, this is years ago — you know what I do? You know I'm a pastor? ... So one time, a dismal Leaf game on a Saturday night and, going to bed, and I say to my wife, "I don't know if I can preach tomorrow after that game." [Laughs] So I mean, it was a joke, but there was some truth to it in the sense that you live and die at some level with the team and so even at this stage, years later, having gone through all the roller coasters, I just hated last year when ... I thought we were on the way to post-season and then they went into the tank ... As much as I would like to be more mature and say that it doesn't affect me at all, it does.

Paul is not the first person to use the language of life and death to describe how he feels about a team, even if it is partly in jest. There is a rhetorical tenor to his diction — "hated," "dismal," emotional "roller coasters" — that evinces how deeply invested he is in the team. Even when he chooses not to watch games, it seems, it is more a function of how much he cares than how little:

Actually, honestly, right now, I don't watch a lot of games. For instance, I get up early, early in the morning, first thing I do is I [go] on my cell phone and look at the scores and [laughs] that's kind of the way that I start the day. So the interest is there. I mean, one of the things that's interesting, my wife believes that I can't stand the pressure anymore because I actually find, when, whatever the sport, things go negatively in a serious way, I immediately want to turn it off because I can't handle watching it unfold any further and then maybe I'll turn it on hoping that there's been some turnaround and sometimes there is but most times there hasn't been.

Paul's wife's rationale is interesting because it suggests just how deeply he experiences the ups and downs of his team's performance. He elaborates on what he was actually feeling in those moments:

Paul: *Well, I think in general I'm relatively optimistic about life things, but in sports I'm a huge pessimist and I know things are going to go badly, and so I hate to supervise and watch them unfold and so if I feel what I think is a trend, a negative trend I'm talking about, it's no surprise to me because I was expecting it to happen anyway. And then, when it does appear to be happening, I'm sad, feel somewhat, you know, I knew it, that kind of, and a little bit mad. Those guys. Wha-? Wha-? I, you know, you do wonder. I don't know how much will has to do in sports, but there certainly seems to be times where there's capitulation on the part of the team that I'm cheering for, and that makes me mad.*

Nathan: *Okay, and there's a lingering sense of that after the game's over?*

Paul: *Yeah, it doesn't, you know, when I get up the next morning, I'm not still usually, in that state. I fortunately did not see the famous game with the Leafs in Boston. Again, but I've heard it's the worst experience in people's lives, and so on. And, I can believe it. I mean, four to one, and whatever number of minutes left in the game, that should have been a done deal. So I think I would have, that might have carried over to the next day. There is regret, especially, now that we're into the playoffs, I, even one game, even a wild card game, at this stage, it would have been fun if the Jays* *could have been there ... there's some lingering, "it would have been grand if they'd done better."*

The intense pessimism of Paul's attitude toward his team differs dramatically from his general disposition towards the world, and perhaps helps to explain how fandom can become a site of condensation for meaning and anxiety in the life of the fan out of proportion with a mere athletic spectacle.

Ashley shows the depth and power of fandom in recounting a rift between her and a friend over attending a sporting event:

> *A friend of mine back in college, he and his family had box seats for the Orioles. And, always, I guess, his mother's family and his father's family had had neighbourhood box seats that were close to each other, so the families throughout the years got to know each other and the mother and father eventually had fallen in love as young people and gotten married. And, so I was friends with the one son, and he was so excited, he said, "I've got, you know, my family has, historically, these box seats. The game's coming up, my family's not going, would you like to go?" And I said, "Sure," because we were very good friends. And, we went, they were excellent seats, and I don't care for baseball ... And so I sat there, and he was getting very into it, and, at one point, the ball almost came our way, and he jumped up to catch it, and it grazed his hands. And, he turned to me, delighted that he'd had this experience, and I was reading a book. I was reading a novel. And he literally, he was so angry and frustrated, he was literally jumping up and down in sort of anger and sort of disbelief that, "Here you are, not only at the game, in these excellent seats that have this history, with me, as a fan, stuff's happening," and I was totally disengaged. Totally disengaged. So there, I think my inability to sort of play along on any level of fandom really was difficult for him. And, it did impact our friendship. We'd only been friends, there was no romantic connection, but it did really impact that because that was something he really liked to do and he was very hurt at my behaviour and my disinterest in his fandom.*

Here we have a close friendship that was disrupted based on a failure to perform the necessary rituals of spectatorship. Yet, instead of indicting her friend for the way he behaved, Ashley seems to empathize with him, as if she might feel similarly if the situation were only slightly altered. This is perhaps because she can relate to the feeling that sport is more than just spectacle in her life:

> *Sometimes I ask myself that after I've watched three hours of a game and I think, "I could have been doing something else 'productive.'" [Whispers] That's a very good question. What do I get out of it? Because, I do, if I put on a hockey game, if I put, especially a football game, I find it very pleasurable. I am content. I will, my body language, you know, I'm on my couch, my feet are up, I have my cat, I have my teapot. I am content. And, there are plenty of other things, in terms of just simple relaxation, there are ways to be occupied. I could put on any show on TV, but ... if I sit and watch a TV show just for the hell of it, just because I don't have something else on the go, I often feel guilty, I feel like I should be doing something productive, I'm wasting my time just watching this show, who cares, mmm ... I don't feel that way when I watch sports and I'm not sure why. I'm really not sure why. Your question's sort of plaguing me now because I can't answer it. I find it enjoyable, I find it pleasurable, but more often than not, if I'm watching sports I'm by myself. So I don't know if it's just easier for me to sort of justify the fact that, yes, I'm occupied doing something, somehow this is more justifiable. But I'm not sure how I would articulate why that's so.*

Ashley finds it difficult to articulate why, in watching sports, she is doing something that does not waste her time, even though her time is something that she values. It does not seem like a reach to say that this is because sports spectatorship fills an essential need, whether it is by reconnecting her to her grandfather, who taught her to love the game, or a broader sense of community; it makes her feel like a part of something. Thus, unlike television, which simply occupies her leisure time, sports watching reproduces her as a human being and is thus something that is essential, not wasteful. This is a feeling shared by nearly every one of the spectators. Sport is not mere distraction but a profound source of meaning. It fills a void that most find it difficult to put their finger on, but nevertheless acknowledge is there.

CONSOLIDATING THE IMAGINED COMMUNITY

In order for athletic spectacle to transcend the logic of the market, the fan's vicarious membership in the team must be consolidated. This is done through the performance of ritual and the acquisition of impassioned objects. After all, fans are not born with the knowledge that they are members of imagined communities of fandom. They must be socialized into these factories of meaning, and this socialization involves making the abstract concrete. The fantasy that one is part of a team becomes reality when one dons the uniform or other signifier of the team and then performs one's membership in public, amongst other members. Fans receive recognition from their peers and offer reciprocal recognition in return. The imagined community is played out through clothing and cheers, much as the singing of a national anthem reasserts the existence of the nation. Tarik describes the Toronto Blue Jays rituals he shares with a friend:

> Tarik: *You start off, there's a build-up, obviously, you talk about the starters, who's pitching that day. We'll both have gear on. I'll bring my jersey, my hat. He has his jersey and he has this old school, one of those '80s parachute jackets. And, that's when you know it's game day, that's when people say, "Oh, you're going to the Jays tonight." They know. Usually we have a couple of beers before and then we have to have a hot dog from a specific vendor, this really good vendor, after Gate 5. A nice lady, she calls everyone, "Babe." It's part of the experience. She understands that.*

> Nathan: *Would you say that's superstition? Or just that you've worked out which vendor you enjoy going to?*

> Tarik: *No, there's no superstition. I don't really believe that. We kid around about the superstition, but that's something completely different. No, it's just a great vendor and we try to patronize vendors that give something back to the people and are not just profit ... I'm pretty sure she's profit-driven, but there's a secondary feeling that this is an experience and I want to be part of the experience, you know what I mean? Very much like the Blue Jays drummer outside, or the people that sell different, I think it's illegal, but Jays stuff outside. I appreciate their existence there, they add to the game ... So yeah, we usually enter, go to our seats, and we used to have a*

jumbo beer per three inning kind of rit-, it wasn't a, it was a ritual, it wasn't for superstition ... There is a ritual, actually, that I do with other friends. You go to, it's called, it's like the porch in the outfield and you have to see first pitch from there to see if the pitcher is on or not. It's like a direct view to the catcher. It's such a vantage point where you can call the pitch from that angle.

Tarik has many rituals, although he distinguishes these from superstition, which he considers irrational. He does not believe that these rituals affect the outcome of the game. However, they are an important part of the "experience." This speaks to the meaning generated through the social experience of attending and bonding with other fans rather than simply being invested in the outcome of the game, as a more traditional superstition might be.

Team history has a ritualistic quality for William:

If I run into another Habs fan, there's a connection. I mean, yeah, especially if they're more my age, or even if they aren't. I've talked to some younger fans who didn't see the Habs in the '70s, which, they were, you know, a dynasty. They won, what, five years in a row the Stanley Cup? And they had incredible seasons and a fun team to watch, and the history. So when I talk to younger fans about the history and that, it's kind of neat to see their reaction, because they weren't there. If you're talking to a twenty- or a thirty-year-old, they weren't there in the '70s, or weren't old enough to see some of those teams.

History is crucial to the invention of community, for it gives the community a lineage that makes it seem venerable and distinguished rather than arbitrary. William considers it significant to ensure that the younger generation of fans is versed in the history of the Canadiens and takes it upon himself to educate them. In doing so he fleshes out the identity of his imagined community of fandom, giving it a concrete reality. Indeed, it is tradition that drew him to the Canadiens in the first place, even though he grew up in Toronto:

Well, that goes back to the teams that they had and the history. And, you have to bear in mind, I don't know if you're familiar with the situation in Toronto in those days? Harold Ballard? And this is part of it. He never really brought the history into the Gardens as much as the Habs [who] always had nights for players who had retired, they hung banners. Ballard didn't seem to, and guys like David Keon never really went back to the rink because of some of the politics with Ballard. But the teams, the Montreal teams back then, were incredible. They were fun to watch, really good hockey and never disappointed.

William describes the importance of tradition to him even as an emerging fan. The pomp, ceremony, and grandeur of the Habs lured him away from a more likely allegiance to his hometown Leafs.

While ritual certainly provides depth to the imagined community of fandom, superstition takes the investment of meaning to another level. Superstition is ritual endowed with gravity and purpose. Whereas ritual conjures a sense of tradition and history, superstition pushes into a different realm, in which the actions of fans (and players) actually impact the outcome of the game. Superstition is fandom taken to its logical conclusion: it transforms players into avatars for the desires of fans.

Nathan: *Can you describe the typical experience of watching a game for you, what you're doing, thinking, what goes into that?*

William: *There's some superstition ... Where I sit, what I wear. I find if I wear my colours, they don't do well. It's just, it's weird. It's the same with soccer, you know, every time I put on my Giggs jersey, they come out playing lousy, so I think, "Okay, I'll wear it either the day before or the day after." Superstitions. [Laughs] And sometimes, it's crazy how a person would think that's going to affect the whole outcome of the game because of where you're sitting [laughs] or what you're wearing halfway across the world, but nonetheless, there are superstitions with ... Same with the Habs chair. If I move it up to the front of the TV, they don't do well. So it's just, silly little things like that.*

Although she does not expand upon it like William, Maria also mentions that superstition is an important part of her experience of fandom.

Just as ritual, history, and superstition allow fans to perform fandom, so too are impassioned objects a requisite part of what makes the imagined community of fandom come to life. Although typically these objects take the form of hats, uniforms, and the like, William reveals additional possibilities: "I even have a Montreal Forum chair ... So when the Forum shut down and they moved to the Bell Centre, they were auctioning off the chairs, so I got [one] ... I've got a Leafs chair as well."* The chairs are important signifiers of his identity as a fan of the team. They are a way of preserving the history of the team but also of creating a physical connection. Perhaps, in an increasingly digital era, this is an effort to bring the arenas into the home. William is able to connect not just with the place but also with the people who once occupied it, his spectatorial ancestors.

The construction of meaning for fans is based on the premise that the team extends beyond the players. Fans' allegiance extends to the team, above and beyond the players who comprise it. They see themselves as part of the team, not as cheerleaders for the players who wear the jerseys. Even as those individual players change over time, fans remain constant in their devotion to the franchise itself. Tarik has favourite players but is more connected to the team: "There is something about a home team mentality that is very important for me being a fan. If Bautista or Encarnacion were traded, I would be very upset, you know. It's not a life-ender, I don't think it would take me off the team." At the end of the day, the team still comes first. Thomas echoes this position: "Okay, so if Phil Kessel got traded to the Ottawa Senators, or something, I would still be a Leafs fan. I probably wouldn't root for Phil Kessel because he's on a team I don't like." William suggests that he is invested in both players and team, although his example indicates that in fact his affection for players is at least partly predicated on their allegiance to the team: "A bit of both. I mean ... the type of player I like are the ones that are loyal to a team, so Giggs never left United. He swore he'd never play for another team. The only other team he played for was Wales, because he was Welsh." In fact, the team does seem to come first for him, and he believes that players should feel the same way. Implicit in this is the fact that he does not see the players as workers or professionals. Rather, the team is something more sacred and profound, worthy of their steadfast devotion.

---

* The Montreal Forum was the home of the Montreal Canadiens hockey team from 1926–1996. Today the Canadiens play at the Bell Centre. Maple Leaf Gardens was home of the Toronto Maple Leafs hockey team from 1931–1999. Today the Maple Leafs play at the Air Canada Centre.

Ashley's take on Ray Rice,[*] formerly of the Baltimore Ravens, shows that the team is of significantly greater importance than any players:

Yeah, I was going to say, do I feel somehow personally besmirched by that because I'm a fan? ... Yeah, a little bit, yeah. I was recently in Maryland, in the Washington D.C. area visiting my mother and so everything is Ravens purple, purple everywhere, and a lot of people were talking about it, the news, the local news, was a lot of talk about it. I do feel a bit awkward that it's a fandom that I have some closer investment and connection to. But at the same time, it's tricky because we know, I think most people realize, that you have your fandom, and that sort of sits above everything ... And then you have the players certainly constitute the team, but they're not static. ... They're constantly moving in and out. So I think it was a bit of, one hesitates to say black eye, for the fandom, but it was more on the player. I saw it more as a personal or a character issue with the player because I find it really, and this affects my ability to be a good fan, the players keep changing. So sometimes in a season, I get really interested in a player's progression, or devalu- ation, depending, and, all of a sudden they're traded, and then it changes the experience of the game for me. I'm not saying better or worse, it's just different, you have a particular team of people ... come together in a certain way and so I find that compelling, and then, all of a sudden, if that is broken up, I'm a little less compelled. It takes me a while to sort of re-gel with new players. So I think, I have more of an affinity with the team at that level of name and location and colour and mascot, as opposed to individual players, because, I'll be honest with you, initially, when this whole story broke, I had heard sort of dribs and drabs ... I didn't recognize him as a Ravens player, it was just some NFL guy ... Later, I found out it was the Ravens and it was like, "Ooh," it hit me a little close to home, a little bit embarrassed that way, but my initial was, "I don't know who this guys is," I couldn't place him.

---

[*]   In February of 2014, Ray Rice, a running back for the Baltimore Ravens in the National Football League, was arrested and charged with the assault of his fiancée. Soon after, a video of the assault was leaked and the story became an international topic of discussion and debate about domestic violence and sport.

Ashley's investment lies in the team above and beyond individual players. She was not even able to place Ray Rice initially because of her frustration with the fluid nature of roster construction. Her connection is to the "colours" above all. This means that the players themselves can be disposable, but also that perhaps the greater part of her enthusiasm is reserved for those people who wear the colours alongside her and thus share in her community of spectatorship. She goes on to describe how interchangeable players are for her:

> I tend to pay less attention to sort of non-pro string players. So if I'm watching a Marlies game, I have no idea who's on the ice. If I'm watching a Bulldogs game, again, couldn't tell you who's on the ice, no real investment ... I don't really keep tabs on the players, I don't really know the players. You know how some people really watch the draft, and they're just like, "Oh my God, who's going, oh my God, did you see who was traded." Never an interest because I'm not that invested in them personally until they get to be sort of big names. And you've got all those guys on the field, or, on the ice, and they're not all going to be big names.*

Despite her earnest enthusiasm, Ashley feels minimal allegiance to players, who seem to function for her in an almost generic, interchangeable way, revealing how a wide range of experiences of fandom can nevertheless yield significant meanings. Ashley's admission that she is not attentive to the nuances of roster management would no doubt yield a disdainful response from many fans, particularly the more misogynistic ones. Yet, although she does not fit the conventional mould of fandom, she nevertheless experiences a similar degree of affective renewal and satisfaction from participating in imagined communities of fandom.

NECESSARY SACRIFICE

Much as ritual and tradition are necessary for the maintenance of the imagined community of fandom, so too is the conviction that players themselves believe the community is worth dying for. It is essential, from the perspective of fans, for players to play through pain and risk

---

* The Marlies are a minor league, AHL affiliate, of the Toronto Maple Leafs. The Bulldogs were a minor league, AHL affiliate, of the Montreal Canadiens until 2015.

their bodies in order to make the stakes of the game real. Their potential sacrifice confirms the inherent meaning of the sport. In part, sacrificing bodies in sport is connected to an athlete's desire to successfully perform masculinity. Yet there seems to be more to this sacrifice. In the context of fandom, this approach to the game is necessary for its popularity — not just because fans want to see violence and fighting for the purposes of mindless entertainment, but more essentially, because fans want to see that players *care*. Players internalize these strictures, which gives the appearance that it is a masculine ethos that is the root and only cause, when in fact both are likely at play.

The spectators believe that it is important that athletes play through pain and risk injury. They consistently view it as a desirable attribute. Mason, for instance, admires athletes willing to endure pain in order to produce for their team:

> *I think it's very interesting that hockey's one of those sports where you get an injury or you hear about all these injuries happening, about people playing through them. It's seen as one of the, I don't want to say, tougher sports, but it's seen as the ones you kind of play through the pain. I wouldn't say that's important to me, but it shows the players' passion that they have, that they want to keep striving. If you get injured on the ice, when you're raised to play hockey, if you get a slap shot in the knee, and you can't really stand on it, you're told to stay on the ice until the whistle goes. You're not told to lie down or, skate over to the bench, you're going to play through the pain. And so that, to me, it's not important, but it's awesome to see people still have that passion throughout their lives for the game to really want to support their team and not give up.*

Although Mason does not want to say that it's "important" to him that people play through injuries, he admires hockey players' willingness to do so; it's one of the things that makes him care about the sport. Mason appreciates the game precisely because of the sacrifice players are willing to make, and it seems possible that his enthusiasm for hockey would be diminished if players did not "play through the pain." This becomes even more evident in his description of an injury he witnessed to the player Steve Stamkos:

Steve Stamkos broke his tibia. He, obviously, going into the post at full speed and just snapping his tibia, that was … one thing, because, again, the injury, the type of hockey player he is, he breaks his tibia, you pretty much broke your leg and he's still trying to stand up to skate off the ice or skate off the pain. You watch that and you understand that these guys are giving one hundred and ten percent. But watching that, you really understand how dangerous the game is, and what you put your body through and sacrifice for this entertainment, for themselves as well as for the fans. I actually grew up in the same city as Steve Stamkos and played with him a few times, so knowing him as a person as well I think affected me a little bit more too, knowing that potentially his career was over because of this injury. But just hoping he's okay and be able to just walk again, let alone, no one cares, once you get injured, people don't care if you're going to play hockey again. They're more concerned, is this guy going to be okay for the rest of his life and that's the scariest moment, is when you see these guys go down and go, "Holy crap, they may not be able to walk again."

While Mason describes being disturbed by the injury and the concern that the player might not be able to play again, he also admires him for it. His description reads as an endorsement of the stakes of professional hockey.

William prizes player loyalty to a team in the athletes he follows. Like the willingness to play through pain, loyalty contributes to the inherent value of the imagined community of fandom. If players are loyal, there must be a reason for this, namely that the team is in some way sacred:

There's a couple of guys on the Habs, but one of the guys, he's only been playing for a couple of years — Gallagher. And, I just like his style of play and he's not a big guy and he just plays like a big guy. And, I think one of the reasons I pick a player is more than just because they can score goals, it has to do with personality and loyalty and not someone who is just there for the money. Some of the guys, it's all about them, and some of the guys, it's all about the team. And there are a couple of guys on United, like Scholes and Giggs, who have since retired, but they played, they went through the whole system of United, played for United, didn't play for anyone else. And, to me, I respect that, that's the type of player

I like. There's some guys that played for the Habs back in the day that never played for anyone else ... But you know, you wonder if Carey Price will stay with Montreal for the long term. You know, a guy like Gallagher, lots of people like him, but he's young and new to the team. You don't see it as often, but when you do, it's really refreshing ... One of the reasons my son watches a lot of sports, not as much as me, he played a lot of sports too, but he enjoys college ball, whether it's basketball, football, hockey. The reason he likes that is because it's more raw. And, those guys, they're not professionals and they're playing, of course, to become professional and make a good salary, but their goals are slightly different than professionals, I think ... He doesn't enjoy watching the NFL *as much, or the* NHL, *or* NBA *[National Basketball Association] because of the fact that there's money involved and it seems to change their attitude. "Oh, I've made it," so to speak.*

The broader story here is about how the team should be treated as something more than just a business. It is framed as sacred; professional sports deface this idealistic fantasy. It is not difficult to see how the context of neoliberalism has resulted in this way of thinking. In a world defined by the bottom line, fans are desperate for something more meaningful and profound. Players who remind them of the corporate nature of sport shatter this illusion, much like the athlete who refuses to play while hurt. Conversely, those who sacrifice themselves for the team are deified as heroes and exemplars. It is wholly consistent with this mentality that William also places particular value on the willingness to play through pain:

Well, it depends on the injury. There's some guys that seem injury-prone or get a little, they have a low pain tolerance or threshold [chuckles], and they have little nagging injuries. I mean, you really can't tell whether it's bad or not, but there's others where you think, "Well, maybe they should sit out." It depends on the type of injury ... It's interesting, because, I watch soccer and then I watch hockey, and I've seen a guy take, they're wearing shin guards and he takes a little knock in the shin and he goes down like he's been shot, rolls around and gets stretchered off, all to draw, you know, a foul, maybe a card, or whatever. Then I watch hockey, and a guy takes a hundred mile an hour slap shot on the ankle and finishes

the play and skates off, and he's got a fractured ankle or whatever,
foot, but he finishes the play, doesn't get stretchered off, generally.
Those guys kind of hobble off and then they find out, "Oh yeah,
it's a, you know, small fracture in his foot," or, whatever, or a deep
contusion, or something like that. And so I guess it's all relative, it's
all theatrics in soccer, and unfortunately it's starting to creep into
hockey but it's one of those things where you don't want to see it
too often. I wish they cracked down on it in soccer because it's a
bit farcical at times, where you think, "What if a guy's really hurt?"

No doubt masculinity is part of the general expectation that athletes should play through pain, but so too is the desire for athletes to sacrifice for the imagined community of fandom. "The theatrics" of soccer that are "starting to creep into hockey" threaten the necessary fiction that the sport is more than just a game. Overly dramatic and implausible behaviour in response to physical contact spoils the illusion that sport is contested for life-and-death stakes. It is the players who play through leg fractures who sustain this fiction and are consequently admirable. This perspective is shared by Linda. When asked which characteristics she admires in a player, she responds, "Somebody who's more of a grinder, or, you know, gets in and gets dirty goals and is persistent and things, those things I appreciate, because that's a high level of compete, and that's where I'm excited, that's what I like to see." This all accords with the fact that fans are interested in seeing players who are perceived to try hard, because they legitimize the value and meaning of the games they are contesting. Not to try is to reveal the arbitrary nature of the activity. Paul has much the same take when asked how athletes should behave: "Well, I like whole-heartedness, I like them to really try hard. I don't expect them to deliver always. So the get-it-done sort of mentality, I don't care how you do it." It is clear that for him it is effort more than results that matter:

So as to how I expect them to try. I don't like to see a guy jog down
to first base. I want to see him run it out, you never know what's
going to happen. And, I love to see guys dive for balls, or whatever,
extend themselves, put themselves in harm's way even, in order to,
for the sake of doing what's required. I like guys who are journey-
men, who dig it out in the corners and don't necessarily score the
goals, so I think trying, whole-heartedness, is big in my view.

Win or lose, it is the effort of the athlete that produces the imagined community of fandom, and it is the existence of the community, more than the satisfaction of vicarious triumph, that provides the fan with a sense of meaning and purpose. The harder players try, the more real the imagined community becomes.

Ashley demonstrates a visceral sense of frustration at the prospect of a player not playing as hard as he can when she has paid money to attend a game:

> I remember, we had tickets once, they were two-hundred-and-fifty dollar tickets, far beyond what I could ever afford at this point, and it was an awful game. It was shameful … It's one thing to see people making an effort and you know they've just been bested by the other team. That's a skill thing and I don't become frustrated in them. I become disappointed for the team, I become a little embarrassed for the team, but I'm not disappointed. I don't think, "Oh, I've wasted my money or my time," or anything like that. But when you're sitting there and you get the feeling that the team just really doesn't give a damn or they're not, as I said earlier, hungry, that they're not committed to being there or whatever, that's when I start to really disengage and get frustrated and annoyed. It's not simply, "I paid my money, I want my experience." It's, I want, I think, on some level, to share in that hunger. I want to be able to sort of project myself as that athlete on the ice and enjoy that challenge and when they're not really, or when I perceive that they're not committed or they seem lazy or slow, or just distracted. You know, every now and then you see a guy on the ice and the puck goes right by him and you're like, "You were not even looking! You twinked-out for a minute, right, what happened?" That drives me wild. I feel almost a little personally offended, you know? You are professional, you are getting, in most cases, a really good paycheque, I realize it's a tough game, I realize physically your body some days is just not at a hundred percent, whatever, and we're all aging [laughs], all that kind of stuff, but at least, give good game, you know? And, if I don't feel I've been given good game, I'm, yeah, I'm frustrated. There's only been one time that my friend Brittany and I, we left early because we were like, "You guys, you're bringing nothing." And you can feel

all the fans get angry, everybody gets angry. And I don't think it's necessarily because they're losing. It's because you're sitting there going, "For God's sake shoot the puck, stop passing it, stop passing the puck," and they just do it and you're just like, "Well, there goes the puck to the other team, great." Right? See, I'm even getting frustrated now just talking, thinking about it!

If the player does not play as if they are hungry, the game starts to feel meaningless. This is not just an issue of being cheated out of the cost of admission. It is an issue of undermining the very legitimacy of the game and the community devoted to it. Ashley elaborates:

I do expect that they are athletes, so I expect them to be properly trained and I expect them to look after themselves, I expect them to do whatever they're supposed to do to prevent injuries in terms of their training, not just to know the plays and the games and stuff like that. So going into the game, stuff happens. It's really complex, how do I feel about that [sighs]? I don't like to see players injured, period. Partly, I fret about them. And it also stops the game and it sort of takes you out of that, right, so that is a little, I don't want to say frustrating, but a little frustrating, because it becomes a distraction. "What's going on with Bob on the sidelines," right? And then it changes the dynamic of the team and the special teams and stuff like that because all of a sudden you've lost somebody, so things, you can see all the guys coming on and off and everybody's sort of talking into their wrists, and saying, "What are we doing now?" I find that just a little distracting. But how do I feel about really playing through an injury? If it's minor, I think I'm okay with that. Because I think we've all done that, if you stub your toe, you still have to, you know, walk from the bus to your house, you just can't check out on the bus [laughs] … I think it's part of my expectation insofar as when I first encountered football, which would have been in the '70s with my grandfather, the real thing was play through the pain. It didn't matter what happened, we have some steroids here and we're gonna get you ready, and off you go. I saw that happen so often, I think I got the impression that [laughs] with steroids, anything is possible. So if they just pumped you enough that you could make it through and that that was okay because you were an athlete and you were committed, right, you had follow-through, you weren't a quitter, right, nobody likes a quitter. I think that played into some sort of framework that I already had about character-building and how you live your life and that sort of thing. I think I found that appealing that they would play through the pain because I thought, "Wow, they are so dedicated and strong," and I do think that formed some of my opinions about how masculinity can be constructed, what are men, well they're strong, they don't cry, they don't come off the field, they certainly don't if it's a bump or a scratch. Okay, they just tough it out, that's what real men do, look at them [laughs], big, off they go to get hurt again. I think that's all in play, so I think I do have a tacit approval of that, to be honest ... Do I find that pleasurable? I find it satisfying, I wouldn't say pleasurable, I do find it satisfying. There is something about seeing someone male who seems to be performing, because I think a lot of it is performative, strength in a traditionally male way, which is, "I'm gonna beat the crap out of this other guy," or "I'm going to neutralize this other male player." There is something deeply satisfying about that that I can't deny as a female I find kind of thrilling. Does that mean I want to see them, you know, butchered and bloodied and that sort of thing? Absolutely not. Again, with the Theismann break, he couldn't play, but I wouldn't have wanted that level of injury. God, no, I was horrified, I still am. People say, "You wanna see the?" "No, I don't want to see the tape. I watched it. I don't. No, no, no, no, not interested." For really gruesome injuries, like where people are down on the ice or something like that, no, I'm horrified, I'm absolutely horrified, but for more minor injuries, yeah, I think I do expect them to play through, yeah, yeah, now that we're sort of talking about it, yeah, and I do find it satisfying.

Although she feels empathy for injured players, one element of her "frustration" is that it disrupts the flow of the game and also affects a team's ability to perform. This is in line with her views about the interchangeability of players. Further, through socialization, she has come to value and extract some measure of pleasure from sacrifice up to the point of excruciation or horrific injury, in line with her feelings about the hunger of players and her investment in masculinity as a gender norm. It becomes clear that she does expect a significant (albeit not absolute) level of sacrifice from players in order to validate the meaning of the imagined community of fandom and her assumptions about masculinity.

Concomitant with the desire for players to play through pain is the greater level of concern many spectators feel for the fate of the team rather than player when a player is injured. Indeed, the meaning of fandom is so profound that it causes members to abandon the moral compass they are typically guided by. The fate of the team and the meaning of the game come to trump all ethical considerations. Tarik exemplifies this attitude in his various comments about Jose Reyes' severe ankle injury in 2013:*

> I'm thinking of the Jose Reyes ankle injury. It's one of those things, it's like an accident that you can't pull your eyes away, there's just something in us that wants to see it. I think his name is Kevin Ware or something, the one who had that horrific, what's it called, compound fracture? Jesus. That's horrible. Or Anderson Silva. I watch some of that too. I didn't actually see the match, I saw the injury. Both of the last two ones I just saw the injury. Yeah. I'm horrified. It's horrific to see that happen to someone partaking in sports, even if it's a violent sport or if it's a non-violent sport, like in Jose Reyes' or Kevin Ware's case. If it's someone I really like, like Jose Reyes — when he came to the team it was like a breath of fresh air and I was really excited for him being traded here — when it happened I was at my friend's house and we saw it and I saw it happen, and my reaction was, "Oh, fuck, no, he's done for the season," and my friend was like, "Calm down, we'll be fine," and I said, "No, no, his ankle is fractured, he's done for the season." Now, obviously the caveat is that I would still watch the season, I'd still enjoy it, but we weren't going to win the World Series, we weren't going to go to the playoffs with this. This was such a derailment in my eyes that I definitely lamented over it and was very vocal about how it was horrific and how I thought it was disgusting and, his ankle just all mangled up under him and too about the value that was just lost there to me as a fan and to the franchise economically speaking. And we obviously know what happened to that season.

---

* In 2013, Jose Reyes was the shortstop for the Toronto Blue Jays of MLB.

Although Tarik begins with the horror of witnessing injury, it is interesting how swiftly he segues into the implications of that injury for the team. Even the statement that he is "done for the season," focuses what has occurred around the interests of the team rather than the player (for whom the greater concerns may be a shortened career and long-term pain/diminished ability). This point is hammered home when he adds, "this was such a derailment," to the prospects of the team. When asked about how he followed up on the injury after it occurred, he adds, "I ... followed up just at a topical level, just knowing when he was game-ready and what he was doing to fix his ankle." Simply put, Tarik's preoccupation is with the player's utility to the team rather than his well-being.

Thomas similarly privileges the instrumental value of players to the team: "Injuries really affect the team in terms of how well they do on and off the ice. If a captain gets injured, usually the team isn't playing at its peak performance because the captain is such a huge part of the team." He does add that he has concerns about injury and prefers to see players sit out than play through it. Yet, the first thing that comes to his mind is the impact of injury on team performance. Even for those fans who care more than most about the individual well-being of players, there is something inherent in fandom that brings them back to the question of team performance first:

It's important that players play through injuries that they can play on. I personally feel that if a player is hopped-up full of painkillers and, say, their ankle is wrapped up if they have an ankle injury or a leg injury, that they shouldn't be playing on it, because not only are they damaging their body, but they're risking the well-being of the team. And there are a lot of legal complications with that as well. And, as someone who has looked into a little bit of that, players who play injured risk losing their entire career if they mess up. A lot of these players have dedicated their entire lives to playing hockey, and one ankle injury is the difference between sitting out half a season and becoming a construction worker because they can't skate. So it's a big deal to me that players don't play injured, because sports injuries are different than other injuries. If I roll my ankle, then I might go to work one less shift because my ankle hurts. But if Sidney Crosby rolls his ankle, he shouldn't be skating the next day, because that's his career. This is my job, right? It's different.

Thomas has a high degree of empathy for what players go through, but he inserts the caveat that it is "risking the well-being of the team."

William views the welfare of the team as paramount. When asked how much attention he pays to injury when watching sports, he replies, "Well, obviously, with this last playoff round with the Habs, they lost their number one goalie. So you pay a lot of attention to it because, it depends on, well, I shouldn't say, [laughs] it depends on who gets injured." Again, it is clear that the focus is on the team. Injuries are worthy of attention when they affect crucial players because the absence of stars jeopardizes the team's performance. His laughter shows an awareness that this may be a callous way of thinking about damage to the body, but it does not prevent him from acknowledging how he feels. The body of the athlete is a vessel for the transmission of meaning. This transfer is complicated when there is no suitable replacement at hand to carry the fan's vicarious aspirations:

> Yeah, it affects the game ... I pay a lot of attention. I mean, going into a game, and going to soccer, I look at the line-up going in because it makes a difference. More so in soccer, because those guys play three-quarters of the game, whoever starts the game and, and if you don't start the right people, or you don't have the people to start, then you just worry about how that might affect the outcome of the game, so if Rooney is not playing, or Giggs wasn't playing or there was an injury to the goalie, I mean, the keeper is important too.

This team-centric utilitarian rationale towards injury is echoed by Maria:

> It affects the team, it really does. Because, the team has its line-ups, the team has its players that they work well with and if that piece of the puzzle is missing, then sometimes it really affects either the morale of the team or it affects the way a line is played, or if you bring a third-liner up to second line then he might not be ready for that. So I follow it pretty closely and want to know when the guy's coming back. Some players, I don't even want them to come back because without them, the Leafs have a funny thing about players who are good on the Marlies, instead of bringing them up they'll put him down there and once a person's injured they'll bring the guy up and he'll score his goals, get some assists and do really well

and work really well with someone, but the minute the injured guy
comes back, he's down. I get it. It's contractual, it's my spot on the
team, etc. But … the fans want wins, they don't want losses all the
time, so you know, and injuries either make them better or make
them worse.

Maria's focus is entirely on the instrumental impact of injuries upon the
team's ability to excel, not the harm done to players' bodies.

Linda identifies less strongly as a fan of any particular professional
team. Nevertheless, her approach to injury also favours the interests of
the team almost entirely over the well-being of the player:

Losing a player to an injury really has an impact on that team,
especially when it's somebody out of those first two lines. But I
think it's sort of at the moment of losing, I have the, "Oh shit, here it
goes," moment, then there's the, "Oh, let's see how long they're going
to be out," and then I don't give it a lot of thought until sort of the
period where they start talking about, "Maybe they're going to be
back." … I have a friend of mine who's, actually, had a good NHL
career, but was plagued by injuries. So I'm a little more personally
sympathetic to how frustrating that is.

Despite being less invested in the team and despite personal connections to professional players in her own life, Linda's focus is almost entirely
on the needs of the team. Her concern is for how long a player will be
out of the line-up. Thus, although she resists the idea of players playing
through injuries, it is not because she worries about what the implications
of doing so will be for their lives:

If you're injured, I mean, there's being sore and tired and a bit
strained, and then there's being injured. No, they're investments.
These players are a business commodity, so I understand that play-
ing through some injuries is acceptable, depending on what they
are, but teams protect their investments. There's a reason people
are out for significant periods of time, even after a concussion you
think, "Well, maybe, maybe they can come back." I do appreciate
that, and I said with the NHL, because lower levels and other areas,
if you're looking at the Olympics and things like that, tend to take

injuries a lot more seriously. Because, with the Olympics, these are NHL *commodities, so they're not going to sacrifice them for that. And, with the lower levels, they just treat it with more seriousness because I think that we've developed a culture where we understand now how devastating concussions and things like that can be. So I don't think it's that important. I think it's probably more important to build a stronger team so that an injury or two doesn't devastate and you can have people rehabilitate properly.*

Although Linda is unequivocally resistant to the idea of players playing through injuries, her reasons for this are grounded in the logic that teams should protect their "investments."

Membership in the imagined community of fandom often confronts fans with ethical dilemmas. Because they are invested in the team and community, they frequently prioritize team success — winning. Yet sometimes the players do not live up to the ethical standards of fans. This places fans in the position of having to cheer for someone they find morally dubious. What is noteworthy about this dilemma is that fans consistently seem to resolve it by choosing to support the player and team. When push comes to shove, the imagined community of fandom is too important to sacrifice to external notions of morality. Thomas articulates this struggle in his response to the player Todd Bertuzzi:

There was a huge injury that happened a long time ago. There's a player, Todd Bertuzzi, who checked from behind this other player, Shawn Moore, and he paralyzed him. And there was a huge issue with that. And I remember watching that game live. When I was watching it, I was, maybe nine or ten years old, maybe eleven, and I remember being upset because I liked Todd Bertuzzi and as soon as that happened I started to think, "Wow, this player isn't the person I thought he was. He's not that kind of role model, upstanding player, he does things like this. I'm not sure if I like him now." And, I remember feeling upset for the other guy, Shawn Moore, because as soon as he went down and didn't get up I had this feeling in the pit of my stomach, "This guy's not okay. This guy's seriously injured." And, as the legal battle continued, and the players were in the media, I remember developing this really big disliking for Todd Bertuzzi for doing that hit, because as the replays showed, there was absolutely no reason for him to hit him aside [from] just being angry. And it's a side note, but now Todd Bertuzzi is part of the Red Wings. And, I have mixed feelings about that as a Red Wings fan, because part of me is like, "He's a good player. Minus all of the bad stuff that he has done, bottom line, he's a good player, he puts up points, he's really good, he fits in with the team." But I can't ignore the fact that he should be in jail for what he did. So there's mixed feelings about those kind of injuries.

Thomas's story shows the difficulty fans can have supporting individual players on a team they cheer for. On the one hand, Thomas deplores Bertuzzi as a human being for what he did. Yet, "bottom line, he's a good player, he puts up points, he's really good, he fits with the team." In the end, the interests of the team weigh at least as heavily as his general philosophy and ethics. This, again, illustrates the abundance of meaning provided by sports fandom. On an emotional level, it transcends other considerations. Mason comes to a similar resolution on the issue of concussions, which he understands to be a significant health risk to athletes:

Nathan: *Is it possible that injuries or new information about injuries would ever stop you from watching hockey?*

Mason: *I'd say at the current state, no. But I think, depending on, because they're really talking about concussions a lot more in the last five years, about how it affects players, and especially the fight-ers of the league, how there's been about three suicides in the last five years, about the brute forces of the league, and the sacrifices that they make mentally and physically, I think, over time, if the information about this really starts growing at the exponential rate that it could, down the line, really just affect the league in general, not just me, but how the game is played. And, so I can see that maybe affecting me. If the sport is on, I know I won't turn away from it, but I think over time the game is going to be changing and that may turn me, if the game is not the same game anymore, that might happen, but right now I don't really see that happening.*

Despite the damning literature on concussions, and Mason's awareness that this has led people to take their own lives, he is not able to turn off the game. William responds to the same question in much the same spirit:

No, I don't think so. I don't think so at all. I would hope that they're going through the concussion thing for a lot of sports. Re-thinking all the rules and equipment and, for example, with hockey, they have the quiet room where they, if they're a little wobbly on the ice, they take them off and they have to examine them and then get a professional to look them over and, whereas before the, and same with football, coach says, "You okay to go?" You know? "Come on, hurry up, we need you back on the field!" [Chuckles] That sort of thing. There's none of that anymore, I mean, they take it a lot more seriously because guys were getting five or six concussions over their career and now they're, I won't say brain dead, but they're complicated, problems with their, not just headaches, but you know, severe, over the years, it's deteriorating. So I think, just, you hope they keep re-inventing the equipment so that it protects the players, and I hope they continue to do and play as they are. I think with hockey it's getting faster and the guys are bigger, so they have to adapt the rules and equipment and they're doing that, you just hope they speed up the process so that, you know, but I think the players are more protected now than they were. It's just catching up.

Although William appears acquainted with recent discourse on injury and sport, he continues to accept the legitimacy of sport as an institution.

It is important to acknowledge that not all fans are willing to put the meaning they draw from the imagined community of fandom over the health and safety of the athletes who animate it. Indeed, for some fans, the well-being of athletic labourers in the face of a sport and culture that demand them to sacrifice their bodies is a source of significant ambivalence and consternation. Paul expresses this sentiment clearly when asked if it is important for him that players play through injuries:

No. I'm very touched by the whole head injury thing. I don't like it when it appears, and I saw a game recently, I forgot what sport, but it sure appeared to me that the person had a concussion and they were out and I couldn't believe it that … I think there was a lot of ignorance, and certainly, getting your bell rung was a saying in hockey and you expected it, and you expected to play through and we loved it when Bobby Bonn scored a goal with a broken foot and stuff. But I would say that my attitudes have changed quite a bit in that regard. I think maybe I did, in earlier years, admire the playing through the injury. At this stage, I, you know, a) I feel it's the responsibility of the team to not allow a person to try to do that; and b) I think the athletes should be honest. I realize that their big fear is that somebody else is going to come up and they'll never get back ... and I feel bad about that. One of the things I noticed about the Canadiens over the years, is all the goalies came up in the playoffs when somebody else got injured and the other one never got to play, back, you know? There's a long run of goalies in the Canadiens, now, I didn't cheer for them, but I still didn't like it, I felt badly for the guy who got squeezed out. So I think, I'm a little bit conflicted, I want the person to get better, but I'd like them to have a chance to play again and I don't really love it when a team never lets them back.

This is perhaps the clearest statement of empathy for what players go through that I encountered. Paul admits to the inclination of wanting them to return, but he does not think that is for the best and feels real concern for what happens to them as a result of playing through injury, a point he elaborates on when asked about whether he would ever give up watching sports because of injury:

I think, if I was watching a game and a fight broke out and I saw a guy get hit and he hit his head, and he was killed, I think that would have a profound effect on me. Now, it's come close and I'm still watching. But I was grossed out, I was appalled and I think that might, I mean, I've never been a person who, for instance, the fact that strikes, you know, seasons are cancelled and so on, I don't vow that I'll never watch again, because I know I will ... But I think if something happened which was related to an injury when in fact the sport had the capacity to prevent it and didn't, and actually seemed to, in a way, promote this kind of activity, that might cause me to decide I can't watch this, even although I love it. You know, I might have to decide not to.

Paul is really the only spectator in this study willing to concede that he probably would stop watching the games if something truly grievous were to occur on his watch.

Ashley displays a similar degree of empathy, despite also extolling players who are willing to play through pain:

I find it really upsetting. I don't know, I think my own nature is somewhat empathetic, so I think that's at play, but I worry, I fret. And, I don't know why, because it's not like it's my son or my husband or my friend on the ice, or on the field. It's not like, also a manager might be concerned, like, "Oh, there's my meal ticket," right? I don't have that sort of investment. It's just enjoyment and entertainment. But yeah, I do hate to see someone hurt. And some of the injuries are quite gruesome, you know? Every now and then you see someone and you can tell that they're, they took a bad hit or they're injured, but they're not injured badly, and that, I'm concerned but I'm not disturbed. But sometimes you'll see injuries where these guys are really hurt, or you don't know, or they're knocked out and you just don't know or they're bleeding on the ice and I think, "Oh, that's really nasty, what's going on?" And, sometimes they play through it and, yeah, I don't know how they do that. I just find it disturbing. I think I'm worried they're going to get more hurt, I think I worry about their future, because if they're really badly injured, then there goes their meal ticket.

Like Paul, Ashley demonstrates concern for players who are injured in sport. Although she relishes the imagined community of fandom, this does not cause her to lose sight of the fact that a complete sacrifice of the athlete's body is not justified by sporting pursuits.

What these exceptions prove more than anything is the rule that for the most part, spectators feel little concern over injuries to the athletes they follow. Indeed, very often they exult in the pain and harm that athletes are subjected to because it validates the overarching meaning and purpose associated with professional sport. For fans, sport is something more than spectacle or distraction. It is a site of profound meaning and purpose that enriches their lives. The question that we must now ask is precisely what form this meaning takes. Why is it that professional sport is able to provide the excess of meaning that is able to inspire such unwavering devotion, devotion that far exceeds any more everyday form of brand or consumer loyalty? The answer to this question has everything to do with the imagined community of fandom and the sense of collective membership and connection associated with it, connection that is exceptionally difficult to achieve in the isolating and alienating conditions of contemporary capitalism.

CHAPTER 4

IMAGINED COMMUNITIES OF FANDOM

For fans, the meaning generated by sport is fundamentally linked to the sense of community it provides, community that compensates for the isolation of capitalist life. This disconnected existence is socialized as natural, so people tend not to see their lives as lacking something essential. But the evidence of this craving for community can be found in the particular pleasure people take in community when they find it. This is why there is such an excess of meaning associated with fandom: the team provides the scaffolding for the construction of an imagined community. Yet the imagined community of athletic fandom is not immune to problems that mar all imagined communities, such as xenophobia, misogyny, and racism. In addition, there is a sort of con inherent in the imagined community of fandom. Although it produces a (fleeting) sense of meaning and connection, it does not provide the foundation for genuine relationships or political solidarity that might lead to social change. Instead, it functions in a distracting manner to sustain capitalism by providing people with just enough emotional sustenance to continue to live the status quo.

CONNECTION

For nearly every spectator, one of the principal sources of satisfaction derived from fandom is a sense of connection to other fans of their chosen team. Thomas describes this:

> *I feel connected to pretty much every Leaf fan because we've all experienced the same thing. I mean, they haven't won in forty odd*

years, so there's this solidarity with Leaf fans where it's like, "this is our year," we want to see them win so bad. In terms of Red Wing fans, I only really know two or three others personally, so I don't really feel that kind of connection. But when I went to a game in Detroit I felt this connection that I hadn't experienced with that team because all of these people who are, maybe they're not locals, but they all came to the game. They're wearing jerseys and hats, you kind of feel connected to that. There's this energy.

Thomas emphasizes a strong connection to other fans because of their shared experience of cheering for the same team, which he describes as "solidarity." On Red Wings fandom, he illustrates how it is possible to feel connected despite a lack of personal relations. Although he is barely acquainted with other Red Wings fans, he comes to feel bonded with them through the team signifiers they wear. Most significantly, he tells us that the experience of collective fandom infuses him with "energy." He is re-animated by the connection he feels to other fans. The implication of rejuvenation in his word choice shows the way in which the imagined community of fandom provides something that is lacking. David McNally argues that the pervasiveness of popular culture metaphors around zombie-ism reflect the way in which capitalism relentlessly deadens the experiences of workers.[1] Thomas resists zombification through his fandom, instead experiencing revitalization. This, of course, is good for capitalism. Thomas explains how he was socialized into the community of fandom:

Part of it was growing up with my dad and my two older brothers watching a lot of sports, so I got into it that way. I remember when I was little, my dad got me one of my brother's old hockey sticks and sawed it off so that I could actually use it and play around in the driveway. I played baseball as a little kid, I started off playing t-ball when I was four or five years old. My dad took me to Blue Jay games and Toronto Argonaut games because back in the early '90s tickets were extremely cheap. You could sit in the 500 section for five bucks or six bucks or something [laughs]. Stuff like that. And then, because I started to enjoy it, I started to like go on my own. Nowadays I'll go with my friends. We'll take the Go bus down and we'll go see a Blue Jays game because I've had fun with those kind of experiences.

This is a typical story about early fandom. Thomas was socialized into his love for the teams he supports by the older men in his family who watched and played the games with him. Attending games as a child planted a seed that blossomed in his own adulthood, when he attempts to reproduce his meaningful early experiences. Mason's early socialization as a fan is markedly similar:

> When I became a fan, it just always seemed like I always was one since my dad and mom always watched it … I remember waking up, or watching the game and then staying up late to watch the rest of it, but when I truly remember becoming a fan on my own was when the Leafs did their playoff run in, I think in '98 or '99, and we were up at my cottage watching the game, and all my cousins and stuff were running around playing … That's when I think I really turned on the jets when it came to becoming a Leafs fan.

For both Thomas and Mason, connection to a physical community of fans was an important part of their development as young fans. While this community initially entailed a concrete relation to nuclear family, they now seek a more intense and gratifying substitute in a community of fans, whether that be in the stadiums of professional sport or in the pleasure of consolidating relations with extended family through shared fandom. Like Thomas and Mason, Maria's early socialization as a fan was informed by the allure of collective investment in a real community. For her it was, "Playing hockey in the schoolyard with friends. And then it domino effected from there and then they would talk about Leafs and then I would get into it."

Community and connection are also central to Mason's experience of fandom:

> Recently, in the last eight months, I've joined a couple different hockey teams and found people who are Leafs fans and ended up talking to them a bit more because of that and a lot of the relationship with them is actually just going to watch the games, have a few beers, and stuff like that, and then that's pretty much it. So the relationship is almost solely based upon our connection through hockey … I'd say that it's a small proportion [of the relationships in my life], maybe 25 percent tops, but those are newer ones.

Although Mason considers fellow fans to comprise only about a quarter of his friendships, this number is on the rise, suggesting that these dynamics are changing as he ages and becomes more passionate about the team. There is, perhaps, a greater urgency to form these sorts of connections as he becomes an adult and is increasingly submerged in the dynamics of capitalism. However, it is equally significant to note the discrepancy — found in most of the spectators — between the number of friendships predicated on sports fandom and the significance of fandom in their lives. For example, although Mason is passionately devoted to the team, he does not consider a particularly high proportion of his actual relationships to be related to this enthusiasm. While the team and its imagined community are an integral part of his sense of self and meaning, few other members of this imagined community actually participate in his life. The satisfaction he derives from sport is thus not a function of relationships built on sports fandom, but rather from the idea of being part of a larger collective.

For William and Maria too, fandom is defined by membership in an ephemeral collective of fellow spectators, often strangers. William says: "There's a sense of being a part of a team. I guess there's that sense of, I don't know if it's community or it's a pride. There's an attachment ... I don't really care who wins ... it's a little more deep-rooted." Winning and losing, although important as a catalyst for the imagined community of fandom, are in the end secondary to being part of something larger than himself. Maria sees the allure of fandom in similar terms:

> You're with them, you cheer, you get rallied up, you get pumped up, you get excited and it's really good to feel that with other people, especially strangers that you don't know and just having that connectedness, like ... behind your team, win or lose, of course. Because I know Leaf fans are so die hard that it doesn't matter. You get into a crowd and you're going to be cheering and you're going to be shouting and it's just, you defend them totally, right to the death.

The language Maria uses is telling. She suggests that it is exciting to share in fandom with others, "especially strangers." Maria also says that the sense of community matters more than winning or losing. The pain of a loss is temporary, but the sense of empowerment that comes from membership in the community lingers. Maria goes further, although it is obviously a hyperbolic statement: "You defend them totally, right to the death." As Benedict Anderson states, the imagined community is something that many people come to feel a willingness to die for. Maria adds:

We'll pay ridiculous amounts of money to go watch them lose, but it doesn't matter. I don't know, it's just pride maybe, just saying that you're a fan and not caring that other people think that it's ridiculous, and knowing other people are there to kind of back you up. I don't know, it's weird to explain ... because you never think about it, you just are, it's just part of you.

Fandom gives Maria something larger than herself to care about and feel a part of, something that seems innate rather than arbitrary or external. Even Linda, who does not identify as a passionate fan of a particular professional hockey team, is drawn to the collective dimensions of fandom in her own way: "During playoffs and the Olympics and Juniors [I watch games] almost exclusively in bars. It's very much seeking out that heightened community excitement thing ... places where I would say people that I'm a little bit more like-minded congregate. It's a little more mine."

The imagined community of fandom comes to life for Ashley most successfully when the capitalist dimensions of professional sport are less apparent:

The Bulldogs games always have little ancillary things, there's a fifty-fifty draw or there's some little something for some charity, there's always something. And so for those, I love to participate because it's just so homespun. It's not slick, it's not sophisticated, it's sweet ... if I go to a Marlies game and they have things like that, sure, I'll participate. If I go to a Leafs game, no I won't. Because I feel like they don't need my money.

When Ashley attends the games of smaller-scale teams, she feels connected to their "homespun" lack of sophistication. However, she doesn't have that sense at NHL games, which feel too impersonal and corporate. Being a fan of a team on that scale does not seem as authentic. Ashley requires a more personal experience that better approximates a genuine community for the construct of the imagined community to be realized.

Given that a sense of membership and connection is pivotal to fandom, it is only logical that the actual experience of watching games has increasingly become informed by social media. Social networking platforms allow spectators to reach out and connect with other fans — whether or not they are personally acquainted — as they watch games. This simultaneously makes the community feel more real and also satisfies a need for connection. It is a comforting reminder that other fans are out there feeling the same emotions for the same reasons at the same time. It provides reassurance that the fan is no longer isolated and alone. While many spectators speak of social media as an important element of their fandom, Thomas provides the clearest statement of the part it plays:

> *Typically, I'm just sitting in my living room. Television's on ... Usually I'm watching alone, unless it's a really big game ... Because of social media, usually my phone is nearby. Sometimes I'll be texting my friends or I'll be on Twitter, or Tumblr, or Facebook or something. And, sometimes, if I miss something, like the score has changed, I immediately go to my phone to check what people are saying, and sometimes things can get heated that way, because everyone has a lot of different opinions about things.*

Thomas's experience is probably becoming more and more typical. Social media allows fans to feel connected to one another even as they remain both physically and structurally alone.

There is little question that attending live games is the ultimate experience of fandom. To be in the presence of possibly tens of thousands of like-minded spectators is the fullest concretization of the imagined community possible. The very fact of so many people cheering for the same team makes real the sense of membership and identity that fans seek in sports fandom. It is their supreme validation. Thomas says:

> *Well, usually there's a lot of energy. Leaf home games usually sell out, so there's not a lot of empty seats and it's mostly Leaf fans, so the energy is pretty much positive, like "Go Leafs." When the Leafs score at home, the stadium just completely erupts. When someone scores on the Leafs, the stadium, you could hear a pin drop, there's absolutely no noise at all. When they win, it's the same kind of thing, just the energy carries over all the way home. Sometimes you can*

even feel it the next day, because you just remember how awesome
it was to just be there.

As Thomas recounts his experience of attending an average game, he returns again and again to the "energy." The crowd is an environment where all of the habits and motivations of the imagined community are condensed into one place at one time. Thomas is amongst others who brandish the same signifiers of membership for the same cause. Being there provides a lingering sense of rejuvenation. Spectators receive a jolt of "energy" from this otherwise abstract community and carry the sensation back with them into their all-too-often isolated/isolating everyday lives. This is what it means to say that the imagined community of fandom functions as a form of social reproduction.

For Mason, it is the *shared* energy and excitement that make the experience so meaningful. The stadium is simply the home writ large. Both provide the meaning that animates his life:

> *When it's game day, there's a whole kind of buzz throughout the*
> *whole day in the city, everyone's wearing blue and white, so it's*
> *awesome to just be down there, feel the energy and then, so getting*
> *there a little earlier, walking around the arena, watching them prep*
> *the ice and all the videos going up, it's, again, taking in so much*
> *more energy than you would just being at home ... I don't think*
> *there's anything in my life that's quite like it, that has that kind of*
> *energy and ... having that kind of energy is absolutely unbelievable.*

For the imagined community of fandom to counter alienation by offering meaning to spectators, it must feel as real as possible. Since rational explanations cannot account for the investment of meaning in what is essentially a consumer spectacle produced entirely to generate corporate profits, justification must come from an irrational identification. Anne McClintock calls objects that facilitate this identification "fetish signifiers" and "impassioned objects" — physical objects that represent membership in the community of fandom.[2] Such visual signifiers obliterate the need for rational argument.[3] Simply the sight of others wearing team clothing engenders a sense of solidarity. Any objects that signify the existence of the team — and its imagined community — effectively confirm the existence and legitimacy of the community.

Thomas explains that the Toronto Maple Leafs and Detroit Red Wings memorabilia he owns are important to him. Merchandise is a significant part of his experience, not only because it is something that he collects but because it makes him "feel like I'm participating":

> *It's important to me because I want to feel like I'm participating by wearing a jersey and a hat, and a lot of these things I've actually got at games, so there's that sentimental thing where you go to a game, you buy a t-shirt, you buy a hat, you wear it back to the next game. I guess I'm part of that cycle of fandom, if you want to put it that way [laughs].*

Wearing memorabilia makes Thomas feel as if he is part of the team. This feeling lingers as nostalgia that is transferred to the memorabilia itself. Wearing some type of team signifier is an essential part of the rituals associated with attending games:

> *I have like a really old Leaf toque that I'll wear sometimes, or I have a Leafs snapback, like a regular kind of fitted hat ... Sometimes I wear a jersey, sometimes I don't. Most of the time I'll wear team colours if I'm lazy because sometimes I'll be coming from school so I'll just know, okay, I'm going to a Blue Jay game, I'll just find the first blue t-shirt I can find ... And, if I've got some extra money, sometimes I'll just buy something there. So if I see a cool Leaf shirt in the Leaf shop, I just might pick it up there.*

Making a point of wearing team colours and on occasion purchasing team merchandise in the stadium are vital parts of the experience, even when taken for granted.

As Mason says, team paraphernalia aid in the performance of membership in the community, allowing for reciprocal acknowledgment among fans (a necessity in an imagined community):

> *You know, honestly, it's probably just the camaraderie of [the] whole group of people being able to show what team you cheer for instead of just being there in regular clothes watching the game. Being able to show pride in your team among other people who have pride in the team, that's important to me ... Obviously, being on Reddit and being a subscriber to r-Leafs and r-Hockey, I think those, I've never*

met [the] majority of people on any of these sub-Reddits but it's all
an awesome community of people who all share the same passion,
and so I feel really close to the community of fans.

Mason has never met the other members of the community, yet describes them as "awesome" and confidently asserts that they "share the same passion." Memorabilia is a significant tool in this process of identity formation and performance, as it functions as physical evidence of community and shared passion, concrete proof that this ephemeral connection is in fact genuine. Mason sees wearing team signifiers as a central part of the ritual of watching games, sometimes even when he is just watching at home: "I tend to wear that stuff … if I'm going to the game, I'll definitely be doing what I can to show blue and white, but if I'm at home, it's not every game, but when I'm going to the game, I definitely go all out." The fact that he is sometimes inclined to wear the colours in his house indicates even more clearly the significance of team merchandise in his experience of fandom. He is able to tap into the satisfaction he derives from membership in the imagined community, even when the community is physically absent, by donning his colours. Memorabilia is able to invoke the sense of membership in community that is so vital to the experience of fandom.

Maria's investment in these objects is so great that she employs particularly hyperbolic language:

What don't I have, seriously? I've got jerseys, I've got limited edition
jerseys with certificate of authenticities, I've got a Gardens chair,
hats, jackets, winter coats, scarves … Oh my God [sighs], I've got the
banners, little replica banners of the Stanley Cup wins, programs,
tickets still, some autographs, some jerseys that have autographs
on it, I'm sure I have more stuff. I've got a box … If the house is
on fire, I'd be carrying it on my back important [laughs], after my
kids, of course, but it's that important.

Although she struggles to articulate why these items are important to her, she explains that the appeal is, "I don't know, just sense of community." This sense of community, represented by her team merchandise, is so important that she claims she would run into a burning building to save it.

Ashley does not actually own any team merchandise. Yet, this does not mean that it is insignificant to her experience of fandom. She explains why she would like to obtain team paraphernalia:

> *Community. It's fun, it's belonging, it's identification. You can see other people who share your fandom. So that's fun, you connect, even at a really subtle level, you just see, "Okay, I'm wearing this colour, you're wearing this colour, we have something in common," and, it helps create community. Whereas, you see someone in the other colours, you're not necessarily disinterested in them but you don't feel like you have as much in common. So with someone, yeah, if we're wearing the same jersey, I already feel like we're connected in some way.*

Ashley is explicitly aware that she desires fan memorabilia precisely because it will contribute to her sense of "community," "belonging," and "identification." She even elaborates on the process through which the spectator makes the visual connection between the sight of team merchandise and a sense of commonality in addressing the question of whether she feels connected to other fans:

> *Yeah, way connected, way connected. If I go to, let's just say, a game in Hamilton and I see other fans, even though I'm not wearing merchandise, I can see all the people and it enhances the experience because you can tell people's literal investment, that you know people have gone and purchased something and they're wearing it, and they've got their faces painted and they've got a hat, or some people have every single possible bit of merchandise on: they've got a hat and a scarf and mittens and a sign and a jersey and a pin and a coffee holder, you know, all these things [laughs]. I think that makes it kind of fun. Visually it's exciting to see everybody in the colours, and, yeah, I think it fosters community. You already feel connected, you already feel like you share an interest. But it's not just an interest; I mean, if we're all sitting at the game, obviously we're interested, right? It's just as easy to sit at home, and cheaper, and less effort trying to get somewhere and commute or get a parking space or whatever. So why would you actually want to go there? Something really exciting happens when you're with the people at the live event and the clothing and the outfits [are] part of that. I*

find that thrilling to be around other people that are actually dressed up and having fun.

Investing in merchandise — a literal monetary investment — solidifies fandom for Ashley by connecting her to the sense of "energy" circulating in fan communities.

The significance of team merchandise is connected to the way in which Tarik is perceived by other fans:

> *Now it's not the same for me with basketball but I do like collecting baseball jerseys because Skydome, Rogers Centre, that experience is not secondary to the game, it's complementary and that experience is very important just like the game to me is very important. You know, there are certain rituals that you develop and one of them is, obviously, wearing the hat and getting the jerseys. I have jerseys from, like the old, not throwbacks, like original jerseys from the last Blue Jays branding, you know what I mean, the jersey that Bautista wore when he hit 55, Encarnacion came in, that era. I have those because I like those more and the nostalgia factor of having those reaffirms my fandom to players, to people who have been fans of the Blue Jays longer than I have. Do you know what I mean? ... Kind of stake my claim, because I missed '91 and '92, I missed the big Blue Jays wave.*

Having older jerseys "reaffirms [his] fandom" and "stakes [his] claim" to the team. In the eyes of some fans, membership is not automatic; it must be earned. Such a notion of authenticity, rehearsed through the "rituals" of fandom, reinforces the gravity of the community.

Paul echoes this regard for authenticity in the imagined community of fandom (even as he self-reflectively critiques this impulse), yearning to share the experience with those who earn his fellowship through a demonstrated investment in the team:

> *If [my son's] home, I love that. You know, if my son's there, and we're watching the game, and he's so avid and so knowledgeable, it's really fun because ... if I'm with a group where they obviously don't know the sport I find that a little bit irritating. You know, if, by the questions they ask or the comments they make, they show*

that they don't have, in my mind, even a minimal understanding
of the sport, which is ridiculous ...

Collective experience is a significant part of what gives Paul satisfaction, yet it must be an experience of a particular kind. Only people who satisfy his requirements of familiarity with insider knowledge contribute to his experience of fandom. This suggests that a standard exists in his mind for membership in the imagined community and shows that the desire for connection is linked to a clear demarcation between insiders and outsiders. Imagining a community of fans also involves delimiting who is outside of that community. This distinction casts the imagined community of fandom in relief, rendering it concrete, real.

SPECTACLE AND REJUVENATION

Generally, the imagined community of fandom plays a significant role in distracting people from the exploitation, inequality, and isolation fostered by neoliberal capitalism, buttressing the status quo and ensuring that the labour force is sufficiently emotionally enlivened to work productively every day.[4] Occasionally, however, fandom can become *too* obsessive and potentially interferes with the fan as a working person. Tarik explains:

Yeah, I haven't thought about the correlation between not going to,
not applying to master's programs and stuff, which was my ambi-
tion to do in the last couple of years, to this thing in the summer,
because it's only the summer, but it is a possibility that I don't study
as much because I do kill a lot of time watching sports.

Unlike some of the spectators I talked with, Tarik feels as if his fandom interferes with his life in a significant way, actually preventing him from devoting time and energy to professional development he would be otherwise interested in pursuing. Yet, there is a way in which this too is beneficial to capitalism. By siphoning the energy and attention of spectators away from other ambitions in life, the imagined community of fandom also breeds a form of complacency that is useful. Tarik illustrates how the imagined community of spectator sport provides distraction and comfort from the difficulties of life:

I went through a very big break-up a couple of years back, and

I'd still go to the games, I'd still watch. Maybe I wasn't as involved mentally because, obviously my mind was on something else, but it still was part of my life. And there is some escapism. It does give you an opportunity to not think about things for a while. Even if you just go and you're a blank canvas, you're blank-minded, you know what I mean? Just being there, just doing the rituals. Just investing the time not thinking about something bad in your life, that could be something that I've done.

The "rituals" of membership in the community provide a distraction and a site of meaning and investment that offer spectators at least temporary distraction from the difficult conditions of their life, whether these are caused by relationship trauma or financial or work-based struggles. Thomas talks about this too:

If I'm in a really negative place, I might try and fill a void in my life by watching a lot of sports and getting really invested in it ... Probably a couple of years ago, I went through a really bad break up and I invested the rest of my summer following the Blue Jays. Every day, I was watching their games online or finding out the scores, talking to friends, stuff like that.

Likewise, fandom helps Mason to revitalize when his life is at its busiest and most overwhelming: "Most of the time I find that, if I'm so busy doing one thing and I need an escape, hockey will be my go to as my, okay I need a break to do something, so I'll watch the Leaf game or I'll go play hockey. There's definitely ups and downs, and absolutely, and that does happen." Hockey is his "escape" from the rest of his life, offering a sense of liberation or freedom.

When Ashley is confronted with challenges in her life, she too turns to fandom: "In the past year, my husband and I have separated, so obviously, a challenging time emotionally, financially, you name it, right across the board. And work is always challenging just by its very nature. In that period ... I have watched tons more." Sports spectatorship increased dramatically in times of personal difficulty and overwork, which is in some ways counterintuitive. We might expect that in periods of higher workload and diminished leisure time, there would be less time to devote to such a hobby. Yet, these are precisely the moments in which fans do turn to sport, for fandom provides them with the rejuvenation that their chaotic, stressful, emotionally draining lives demand. In Ashley's case it is related to her employment and the toll it takes on her emotional well-being:

> *My training was as a specialist in … [the humanities], so that's what I did my graduate work in. Unfortunately, there are no jobs in that area, so after a lot of soul-searching, I decided to try for a career-switch. Currently I've moved into law, so I work as a legal assistant and a law clerk. Because of my background as an academic and an intellectual I find the work under-stimulating … You watch time-lines, you generate documents, you proof-read. I'm often generating things that need to be bound, you know, so photocopying, binding, punching little holes in things, making big or small booklets. I find that work soul-crushing, to be perfectly candid.*

Given the "soul-crushing" character of Ashley's labour, it is little wonder that she invests so much of herself in her fandom.

The fetishistic quality of the fan community is cast into even clearer relief when juxtaposed with participation in a more authentic form of hockey community — based on concrete as opposed to abstract relations. For those who participate in a more authentic community, the imagined community offers significantly less seductive allure. Linda grew up in a small hockey-obsessed town in British Columbia:

> *My brother was a hockey player, my father was an announcer, my mother ran the booster club. My parents were very involved in fundraising for minor hockey. They had a junior AA team where I grew up, and they had a men's league … I sang anthems. We went to almost every game growing up. I went to school with guys who ended up in the NHL, I was babysat by guys who ended up in the NHL, we were a hockey family. You know, my brother played up through university, so we'd always done it. Most of my memories of being a little kid are Friday, Saturday nights at the rink watching the [local junior team] play. So … it's organic … I grew up watching it. That's what we did … It was a very in-personal experience that didn't actually involve playing hockey.*

The hockey culture in Linda's hometown did not involve watching the sport on television. It meant being at the rink, singing anthems, and going to school with people who played. Linda grew up watching in a more "organic" way that evidently did not prove to be conducive to membership in an imagined community.

US AGAINST THEM

You may wonder why I am dwelling at great length on the ways in which athletic fandom takes the form of an imagined community. If people find solace in sports fandom from the hardship they experience in their lives, isn't this something to applaud, not condemn? Part of the answer to this question can be found in the oppositional dimensions of the imagined community of fandom — its "us against them" way of engaging with the world. In forming a community based on an abstract notion of sameness, fans simultaneously position themselves in opposition to an equally abstract conception of otherness. And, although the foundation of this configuration is abstract, the consequences are concrete and contain the potential for real harm.

Thomas describes how the antagonism of sports fandom resulted in the destruction of personal friendships:

> *Growing up, I had these three really close friends who lived in my neighbourhood ... We all ended up being part of different hockey fans. My one friend, he became a Vancouver Canucks fan ... And, my two other friends ... they really followed the Washington Capitals ... And, I grew up a Leaf fan ... So every once in a while, we'd get into arguments about hockey and stuff like that and eventually, when we stopped playing hockey as well, like road hockey, a little bit of ice hockey and stuff, the friendship completely fizzled out because there was literally nothing left ... And maybe it's too personal, but honestly, I haven't talked to these guys in almost a couple of years now, because there's nothing left. I've sat down and tried to figure it out and there's nothing. It was that.*

Sports fandom can also draw a wedge between strangers, creating antagonistic interactions that would not otherwise exist, especially through the vehicle of social media. William talks about this:

> *With social media, it's made the world smaller, but it's also brought*

in, how do I put it, the conflict ... Other fans that support other teams have a hate for your team ... So a Leaf fan despises Habs fans, or despises the Habs and if you're associated with the Habs ... But it's funny how social media has brought that a little closer, so if you walk down the street, if you're not wearing a Habs jersey, a Leafs fan wouldn't know, right? But if you're on the Habs site and you're supporting your team, you can get a lot of a negative, you know, there's a lot of trolls out there, just bombard you with nasty, nasty stuff.

In the evolution of fandom in the digital age, we might assume that fan networks would weaken when migrated from physical to virtual spaces, but the opposite seems to occur. Antagonisms are heightened and crystallized. Social media magnifies the us-against-them dynamic of the imagined community of fandom and creates an arena for conflict. The fan community itself inspires this conflict for it positions unacquainted individuals who support different teams in opposition with one another, so that the very terms of their relations are defined by difference rather than the potential for solidarity.

Paul, a Maple Leafs fan, is unable to suppress the antagonism he feels through his fandom despite the fact that it diametrically opposes his personal and professional moral code:

In hockey, because an area of my responsibility obviously, for instance, [is] Ottawa [laughs] and, so I actually went to a Senators game with one of our clergy last year and tried really hard to cheer for the Senators because it seemed like the right thing. But it was very hard to do. They were playing the Islanders, so I didn't really care. But when the Islanders won in the shoot-out at the end, I quietly cheered in my heart. I mean, I think that I know that those are sane people that cheer for the Senators and they feel the same way as I do about the Leafs and ... actually, the guy who took me to the game, his two favourite teams are the Senators and the Canucks, both of which would be at the bottom of the list for me in terms of, so I mean, I respect him, I like him [laughs], but we have this sparring relationship where we don't talk about it a whole lot, because as soon as you go a little ways, you discover that you actually feel it a little bit more than you should. [Laughs]

Despite Paul's best attempts to suppress his fandom, "in [his] heart" he cannot overcome his distaste for opposing teams. He is aware that this dislike is irrational, but this fact does not change the way that he feels.

ICE GIRLS

The definition of who can be included in the imagined community of hockey fandom is often further regulated according to gender. Just as society at large in North America privileges white masculine heterosexuality, so too does the fan community. This creates an uncomfortable dynamic for those who seek membership in the community but recognize themselves as not fitting within its homogenous logic. Linda is uneasy about hockey fan culture because of this:

> We were at a game last night, and I find myself looking around and going, "Wow," there's a bit of the white bubba culture to it ... It's a more aggressive, it seems sort of a lower income, which is bizarre because hockey games are so incredibly expensive to attend, lower-educated, suburban, all of the things that sort of reformed hipsters like myself don't necessarily find attractive in a group of people or an audience or a crowd. It's very white. It tends to be fairly male ... So that's a bit of a turn-off for me at times. There's a little bit of rabidness to it that I also find a turn-off, which is probably the reason I never really got into football as much, because I find it's even more so and I find it a little jarring.

Linda is the one spectator I interviewed who consistently positions herself as a relative outsider to any imagined community of fandom. That may have a great deal to do with the composition of the community, of who is allowed in and who is kept out. She critiques the community for its homogenous whiteness and also its "male"-ness. The reference to the masculine nature of the community is not simply a gendered generalization, for she particularly highlights the "aggressive" "rabidness" of the members, hallmarks of hegemonic masculinity.[5] It is a particular version of masculinity that governs the spectatorship of these games, one that is uncomfortable for those who don't identify with this mode of behaviour. As she elaborates, it becomes still more apparent that it is the patriarchal nature of the gender relations embedded in the imagined community of fandom that makes it so difficult for her to invest in it:

The fan culture is more alienating, the way that women are incorporated into the game I don't find appealing. I ... went to the game last night and they've incorporated ice girls (and that's my term, that's certainly not theirs) but it's a bunch of young women, and they're all good-looking women who can skate very, very well wearing crop tops with flowing hair and tiny little skirts dry-scraping the ice between plays and commercial breaks. And, I couldn't help but think to myself, it's kind of like having cheerleaders without having cheerleaders. They're clearly all very good skaters. They're clearly, I mean, they're wearing hockey skates so they're clearly young women who've, I'm assuming, played hockey at some point in time, because hockey skates are a real switch from figure skates, and I couldn't help think to myself, put some damn pants on and maybe incorporate junior teams and women's teams. If you really want to incorporate women into this, do it in a way that isn't, and, I mean, you've used the word "alienating" and I can adopt that use, that isn't alienating or doesn't feel sexist or doesn't feel objectifying. But of course, I'm overthinking it by half already, and these are, I'm not the audience, so you know, otherwise they'd just have a bunch of dudes in sweatpants and warm-ups dry-scraping the ice. So the fact that you see things like the nfl very aggressively trying to incorporate women into their fan base, or to repair some of the damage that's happened because of recent incidents, whether it was domestic violence or child abuse, and what have you. And then I see them come out, the nhl, with their pink jerseys and their ice girls and I think, wow that's not the way to sell it to me. That's maybe the way to sell it to a woman who needs to see the glamour in the sport or is, you know, the pink jersey is someone who is adopting the sport as an activity because they've got a partner who is actually a fan, but it doesn't include me, those moves. So I find the whole thing a little bit odd. The imagined communities of hockey (and likely most pro sports) fandom are not designed for women. They are engineered by the corporations that own professional sports teams according to the assumption that membership is reserved exclusively for heterosexual men who enjoy the objectification of women's bodies. When women enter these spaces, they are expected to perform conventional gender roles by donning a "pink jersey." It may well be that Linda has been unable to fully assimilate herself to the imagined community precisely because of a sense of alienation from its gender dynamics. After all, she is an avid, lifelong hockey fan who enjoys watching games, yet she has not fully immersed herself in the community of any team.

Linda is not the only woman to find the imagined communities of hockey to be hyper-masculine spaces. Ashley grew up in the southern United States:

> *I grew up at a time ... where it was a bit more conservative in terms of views towards women and there was very much a sense that I was being brought up as a lady and that ladies certainly could be fans, but you'd never really, I mean, you would be a fan because your partner would be a fan, of course that's, you know, you'd make sandwiches for the men and they would enjoy the game, but you would never sit there and cheer a team on, because it just wasn't lady-like.*

Ashley's fandom is very much a counter-story to the hegemonic rule that the imagined community of sports spectatorship is not a place in which women can be members (although their labour is essential to its function). There is a role for women in the world of fandom but it is one that is predicated on traditional gender dynamics. Women can exist peripherally to the imagined community as long as they accentuate the experience of the men, who are its "authentic" members, whether that is by objectifying themselves as "ice girls," labouring to provide refreshment, or dutifully acting like traditional cis-gendered heterosexual women in pink jerseys. While the imagined community of fandom compels women to perform traditional femininity, it likewise invites men to perform hegemonic masculinity, as Ashley explains:

> *I had an experience where, it was a Bulldogs game, and there was one guy seated around us with his buddies and just progressively got more and more inebriated ... and so just started picking on people ... and he was making it really uncomfortable. You're in a crowd with, seemed to be predominantly men, and many of them were drinking and so you could see it was just escalating, because even the other men who were being picked on who weren't as inebriated as this guy felt the need to sort of rise to the challenge and put this guy in his place. You know, finally security showed up.*

Hegemonic masculinity is the predominant form of gender expression in these places. Ashley describes an environment in which increasingly intoxicated men aggressively vie with one another to prove who is the most masculine, a situation that leaves her literally anxious for her own safety. No less than the pink jerseys and ice girls of Linda's narrative, this macho behaviour demonstrates who is and is not welcome within the imagined community of fandom. This is a community designed for men who identify with conventional and constraining notions of gender and sexuality. If women are to participate, they must align themselves with the same gender logic — indeed, they must participate in their own objectification — or they will be made to feel uncomfortable and unwelcome.

The imagined community of fandom is a principal site of meaning and purpose in the lives of fans, particularly in the face of personal trauma and the rigours of life in an advanced capitalist society. Yet, the imagined community of fandom is not a panacea — it does not actually transform people's lives or significantly help with their problems. Membership requires the cultivation of an us-against-them way of perceiving the world that leads to further division and antagonism. Nor is it equally available for everyone. For female fans, membership is predicated on a willingness to subordinate their marginalized identities to the requirements of the community. Hegemonic masculinity (and whiteness) remain the dominant modes of identity, and homogeneity reigns.

CHAPTER 5

SACRIFICING THE SELF

Spectators derive meaning from the imagined community of fandom, which is entirely contingent on the labour provided by athletes. As we discussed earlier, this athletic work is a form of social reproductive labour precisely because it provides a sense of emotional and psychological revitalization for spectators. The labour of athletes is the foundation for a temporary relief from the isolation of modern capitalism. What, however, is the cost borne by the athletes? Beyond providing labour under the control of team owners, what are the consequences for athletes of producing a source of meaning for fans? That meaning is only possible when the stakes transcend those of a simple game. The imagined community of fandom can only be born in the context of a competition that seems to approach the level of a life or death struggle. Athletes must portray the requisite level of passion, urgency, and desperation to make this imagined community possible. According to many of the athletes I spoke with, the role and responsibility of sustaining the construct of fandom feels unnatural and carries significant emotional and physical costs. It creates an emotional vacuum for players once careers end, by discarding them from their position as vessels of fan adoration. At the same time, their bodies (and minds) are permanently damaged, no longer capable of athletic prowess, or even, sometimes, the banalities of everyday existence. These are the costs athletes must bear for their social reproductive labour within their professional hockey careers and as they move beyond those careers.

ROLE-PLAYING GAMES

To work as a professional athlete is to perform a role for the gratification of spectators. This means that athletes must act in a manner that generates meaning for fans. This role-playing is what the entire political economy of sport hinges upon. The role requires the distortion of an athlete's identity so that it fits the contours demanded by the imagined community of fandom. Sean explains:

> *Most tough guys that I ever met and liked, when your parents meet them or somebody meets them away, he goes, "Wow, I thought you'd be a real a-hole off the ice," right, but really and truly, he's just playing his role and he's just like a bad guy in wrestling. If he's a bad guy, he's probably the guy that's giving the most to charity and giving his time to functions and different events ... But no, outside of the game, you want to have your name as being a good person and being a good guy in society.*

Lawrence elaborates on how the roles that athletes play typically bear little relation to their actual personalities:

> *I'm not a violent man. I'm not about violence ... I'm a passive man who comes from a loving family and I got put in this role of violence, you know, fighting, protecting my teammates. You know, it wasn't me. I hated it ... it was a thing where it wasn't me ... I was almost like a WWE wrestler in a more violent sense. They're different people when they're at home with their kids than they are when they put their trunks on and going into the ring. I put my equipment on and became a different person.*

Lawrence is fully conscious of the way that he was compelled to play a part, particularly in his role as enforcer, a role that required him to instigate and engage in violence on the ice. His reference to a "WWE wrestler," like Sean's reference to "wrestling," suggests that he understands the spectacular nature of the proceedings. Although he does not make the connection that he is actually doing this for fans — giving them something they need or want — he reveals how alienating it was for him to be someone he felt he was not:

Well, it wasn't a good feeling because I was fighting 6'6 monsters every night. The feeling of fear was terrible. The feeling that if I lose badly I'm out of hockey. You're not only fighting, but your, your, your, your life's in danger, your career's in danger, your paycheque's in danger. When, when, you know, when you go out there, as much entertainment as people thinks it is, if I was to go out and get knocked out severely, bad concussion and then end up getting sent to the minors, then, here I am, out of, out of, you know, my whole dream is gone. It was a terrible feeling. I, I, I don't use the word "hate" strongly. I hated it. I hated my role in hockey.

Lawrence was subjected to tremendous emotional strain in his role as enforcer — "the feeling of fear was terrible," "I hated it." On three separate occasions in this short passage he repeats his words, as if he is too agitated to get his ideas out directly. The emotional turmoil he feels is directly connected to the role he had to play, a role that was, in effect, designed to satiate the need of fans for violence by underlining the depth of antagonism between one imagined community and another.

Lawrence also understood how this player role boosted his status as an entertainer:

Yeah, and I also learned when I got beat twice. A [player] beat me up twice in Madison Square Gardens. And it bothered me so much that the fans, who were yelling [his name] and like this whole circus atmosphere, and it bothered me for the longest time. And then, as I got more educated with the fighting role, it was almost like it helped me because of the entertainment value. It was all over ESPN and Sports Desk and I'm looking at it like, "Oh my gosh, look at this," but it actually helped me, because people were going, "Hey did you see, even though you lost, you're this ... " So you've got to look out through the win or the losses of what it did for my career.

Although Lawrence claims to understand better — to have become "more educated" about his role — the strongest sentiment he expresses is how he was "bothered" "so much" and how that stayed with him "the longest time." In fact, even though he was told, right after the event, that it would be beneficial to his career, the impact of the moment lingered with him far longer. This suggests that players come to internalize the logic of the game that tells them it is their responsibility to play a role, while at the same time they struggle with the way they feel about that role. As much as Lawrence came to know it was economically in his best interest and that of the league for him to play a villain and, sometimes a loser, he could not help feeling uncomfortable with this role. His discomfort with the role of villain also speaks to the power of the crowd's adulation. It was something to be fought for, a reward in its own right, which he was "bothered" to lose. We can only wonder what the permanent removal of this powerful intoxicant feels like for every player exposed to it.

Darin also struggled with the burden of fulfilling the role of enforcer: "Well I think that it wasn't, it was nat-, I was naturally good at it, it kept me a job, but my demeanour was not really a mean guy. So for me it was more, turn the switch off or turn the switch on when you get to the rink and turn it off when you leave." He does not elaborate, but evidently the role of enforcer did not feel comfortable or natural. He turned a switch on in order to become the person professional hockey demanded he be.

Curtis's experience was much the same, though he had to transition from being an offensive player to enforcer (a transition, I was told, that most players who end up as enforcers must make): "I didn't like it because it's not, it wasn't me, it wasn't my style ... I assumed I was drafted based on what I had done, so you know, that changed ... that's what they wanted, I just did what I was told to do, basically, at that point." He did not feel comfortable in the new position, saying he was compelled to act as a different person in order to give the team, and fans, what they wanted, at the expense of his own comfort and satisfaction. There is little question that the pressure of knowing that an army of other candidates to take their jobs was a factor in forcing players like Curtis, Darin, and Lawrence to perform a role they did not enjoy or identify with. There is always an awareness in their comments that if they betrayed any reluctance whatsoever, they could have lost their jobs in an instant to one of the thousands of other aspiring professional hockey players willing to do whatever is necessary to take their place.

It is not only enforcers who believe that to work as a professional hockey player is to take on an alienated role. Luc, who enjoyed a more privileged position in the ranks of professional hockey, felt much the same:

If things go well, obviously it facilitates the relations between the athletes and the fans, where everybody is happy. Where it becomes complicated is when the team is not doing well or when you as a player is not performing for different reasons. And they are different reasons why an athlete is not performing all the time, and very often, I would say most of the time, fans don't really know the real reasons why the athletes are not performing. You're watching the games and what you think is that, you know, all the athletes are on the same page and all feeling good, all have lives without problems, but it's never the fact, you know? ... It could be health, it could be injuries, it could be something related to his home life, his family and things like that, and people are not aware of that. I remember at the end of my career, when I was last couple years dealing with lots of injuries, but people are not really aware that you're fighting through all that stuff. For an athlete, it's very hard to perform at its normal level dealing with all that stuff, but meanwhile, the effort and the sacrifice to play is out of this world and it's something that people don't know.

Luc describes the frustration of constantly being in the spotlight, observed and scrutinized by fans, regardless of the specific role a player has on the team. His acute awareness of the attitudes and ideas of fans confirms the strain he was under to give them what they wanted. Fans envision players to be a species of supermen, unencumbered by the frailties that afflict average people, such as pain and exhaustion. It is into these supermen that spectators invest their hopes and aspirations and upon them that they build their imagined community of fandom. This is the role that Luc found so difficult to play, no doubt because it is a role no actual human being could completely satisfy.

Some other players, for instance Vasil, found it easier to fulfil the roles they were asked to play:

My first year of professional hockey, I was named the first star, I think, in my third game, and when I skated out to be the first star, I skated out as fast as I can and I dove on the ice. Ever since that day, I became a fan favourite because of that reason. Because I think they probably knew that I was doing it for them than for anything else. There are a lot of hockey players that keep to [themselves] ... but I was a little bit more outgoing, and the fans really, really enjoyed that … I guess maybe I like the spotlight a little bit too as well, but any place I played, if you look through the teams, I was a popular player because of that reason, because I engaged myself with the fans.

Vasil clearly revels in his role as a fan favourite. Yet, what is common between this and the earlier stories is an awareness that players are expected to play a role for fans. It is this knowledge that causes the player to experience both an abundance of meaning during his career and the loss of that meaning once it is over. Vasil became a fan favourite — and accrued the no doubt deeply satisfying adulation that accompanies that status — because he performed his role impeccably. As we have seen, this is not just a question of wins and losses. Even more significantly, it is about validating the construct of professional hockey as a site of meaning and investment *for the fans.*

Sean, who was a stay-at-home defenceman, shared Vasil's outlook in that he did not find it to be a significant strain to play a part for fans:

There were a couple of seasons where I'd been around for a while, and people had got to know me, again, like, in a smaller town, they'd see you getting groceries … So sometimes you're playing a role. You're, what I'd say, you weren't playing a role, you were just a promoter of your club, so you want to be an outstanding guy to support your club. You didn't want to act like an a-hole because then your reflection of yourself would be to the club. So most of the times it was just being a nice person to what it was. Not fake, I don't want to say fake, but at the end of the day, these are people that you really don't know, you know what I mean? They don't know your family, they don't know your past history. So most of the time, you're just kind of just being polite.

Although Sean does not appear to have found it to be particularly unpleasant, he is highly conscious of the fact that he was expected to play a role. Although the role on the ice might be to play as hard as possible, off the ice he was expected to appease fans. If he were to "act like an a-hole," it might be more difficult for fans to invest in the team. So it was necessary for him to be pleasant at all times. The compulsion to play a role was not merely limited to the moments when they were technically at work on the ice in front of fans. In their capacity as public figures, players are always in the spotlight, which means they are never completely able to escape the demand of performance.

VESSELS OF MEANING

The social reproductive labour of athletes requires them to become "vessels" of meaning for fans. At its most basic level, the imagined community of fandom builds its sense of identity around a team of players playing a sport. Each of these players becomes the physical embodiment of that community and all of its hopes and aspirations. Players experience a remarkable sense of empowerment as they become the locus of meaning for thousands of people in the course of their work. However, once the career ends, or once the athlete becomes injured and is unable to labour on behalf of the community, he is discarded and forgotten, left only with the scars of the meaning inscribed on his body. This is a form of emotional trauma.

Sean explains that to be at the centre of the crowd's adulation, even at the relatively lower level of European professional hockey, made him "feel … special … like [he] was something bigger than what the game was":

> *There were some games when it kicked off and it got a little bit, some fights would happen. Let's say, for example, I wasn't a big time heavy fighter or something, but there would be a game if someone would run your goalie, you'd have to drop your gloves a bit and next thing you'd get kicked off the ice. And, if you were on the road, soon as they would kick you off, they were cheering, booing, this and that and it made me feel … special. It made me feel like I was something bigger than what the game was, you know what I mean? And, I know fighters that couldn't wait, it was almost better to fight away so that they could get booed, and it was almost cooler on that side of things, that everyone hated you. So when it happened to me, occasionally, I used to think it was the coolest thing in the world. Yeah, there was times where you'd score, you felt like a million bucks. There was times, for me, I didn't score much, but I could break up a two-on-one, and they'd react and you'd just get lifted … Somebody could be dying and you wouldn't [care], you just felt so good. You just felt like you wanted that to happen again every, every, every*

time. Those kind of plays that I would do would come along every, maybe, eight games because of the way I played, I was just a steady bee, and no one's reacting by good stick on puck, or winning a battle in the corner, you're not going to get a reaction as a goal-scorer would, but once in a while you'd block a shot and sacrifice your body to block it and the fans would react and you didn't get it all the time, so when you did get it, you really felt special. It was the best feeling in the world. You didn't care about anything else, but in that moment, so yeah.

Sean describes a sense of euphoria, the pinnacle of the moment where the player is showered in adulation so powerful that "somebody could be dying and you wouldn't [care]." These moments were so intoxicating that at the time they validated for him the entire experience of labour in professional hockey. In talking about the potential pressure from fans to play through injury, he returns to what it felt like to be the focal point of meaning for an entire community of people:

I wouldn't think it would be so much the pressure side of the fans to go out there and risk injury to improve, but just that stage, that whole, I mean, again, it's hard for me to explain because it was, no one [laughs] really mattered if I was there or not, but that whole rush, that whole energy rush that you go out there and you can put twelve hundred people or four thousand people on their feet by your play, that's gotta be some kind of want and excitement. That's what keeps guys going in the off-season is can't wait to hear the roar of the fans. The fans help them go, the fans are the ones that keep them energized and keep them focused and keep them, you know, the whole reason why you keep going and playing this game.

Sean moves from a question asking about if he felt pressure from fans to play through injury — he acknowledges that he did feel some pressure to impress fans, as that would have material consequences on his quality of life as a semi-professional in a small European league — to an unprovoked meditation on the emotional gratification that playing in front of fans gave him. This sense of purpose seems to have been a primary form of compensation he received for his efforts and motivated him throughout his career.

Finally, Sean reflects on how often he thinks about his career and what it feels like to no longer be the focal point for the production of meaning:

Every day. I was down in Elmira, New York, for a division three college game, and there was probably about two thousand people there, and it brings you back, doesn't matter where you are in the game, it brings you back to when you played. A certain song can hit on the sound system and you can remember taking a face-off to the song or being somewhere, identifying, because I identify a lot of stuff in hockey to music, because certain warm-up songs, they'd play, like "Small Town" by John Cougar, I mean, they used to play that in [the U.K.] every time you'd go on the ice and it was just a cool warm-up song and, yeah, every time, you'll always miss it. You'll never ever, I mean, you could be fifty years old and still playing and you could retire at fifty-one, at fifty-two you're going to miss it. You always will. Because, not to say you're not important, but you know ... because of the fans and the way they reacted to you was the reason why you missed it.

There is a tremendous sense of nostalgia in Sean's answer, sensual details that trigger powerful memories. For him, this is not about just camaraderie with teammates, but "because of the fans and the way they reacted to you was the reason why you missed it." Remarkably, the sense of loss began almost the instant his career ended. This is the reality of being a professional athlete. The moment a player ceases to be the embodiment of the imagined community of fandom, he is forgotten and another takes his place. Whether this is because of injury or the end of a career, the transition is instantaneous and ruthless.

Darin denies that he would alter the nature of his performance for fans, but he cannot dispute the stimulation he personally felt from being the object of their focus: "I pretty much was myself the whole time. I mean, you can play off the fans as far as getting energy and adrenaline and they get you going. But I wouldn't change my game for them, no." It is worth dwelling on his reference to the "energy and adrenaline" he received from the crowd. This speaks on one level to the way in which players become vessels of meaning. On another, it confirms the existence of a feedback loop in which players and fans supply one another with "energy." Although in the moment this process appears to be mutually beneficial, in the final accounting, the player is fundamentally depleted and altered by an exchange that offers fans little more than a fleeting boost. Darin also talks about what it feels like to no longer be the object of the crowd's affections:

> Well, nobody, you know, it's been nine years since I've played in front of a crowd like that and you know, it's hard to explain, I guess, it's one of the most, or, the biggest thrills a person can have, you know, so when you don't have it anymore, you look back and really sort of go, "Wow, it was pretty awesome to do that."

Darin struggles to find a way to articulate his experience — the magnitude of being the repository of meaning for thousands of people:

> It was a journey. It was an eye-opening journey. You know, moving on from hockey and trying to figure out what you wanted to do ... The first couple of years were tough ... You feel lost without what you had since you were five. You knew you wanted to be a hockey player every day, and then all of a sudden, when the hockey's done, you're not really, you know, you just miss it, you miss the game.

Darin emphasizes that he has lost his identity as an athlete, but it is hard not to think that part of this is also being the object of so much investment, particularly since he references the way in which his culture instills the significance of being a hockey player "every day." It is not just that he has lost the only occupation he has known; it is that this occupation has also been exalted as the height of experience and achievement.

Lawrence also describes missing playing regularly in front of a crowd:

> Well, when you look back ... when it goes, when it leaves, you realize how special it was that twenty thousand people paid to come watch you ... and then when you retire, it's gone. Right, it's over ... When I go out and play ... in NHL alumni games now, and there's a thousand people, it's still entertaining for them to say, "hey, we remember you," right?

Lawrence highlights the abrupt transition from being the focus of meaning and desire for fans to the emptiness when that meaning is transferred to other bodies. It is little wonder that he wishes to feel remembered in alumni games, for the process of retiring is the process of being discarded and forgotten.

While Vasil is nostalgic about playing in front of a crowd, what he misses more is the camaraderie with teammates:

> *The fans kind of pumped me up as well. You know, the national anthem and the fans screaming and the goaltender is the most focused player on the ice, so you make a big save, the fans love you, or you win games for the team, the fans love you ... The biggest thing that I miss the most is just being in the dressing room with the players. You know, you're a tight family. You're with them every single day. I lived with a couple of players too during the season. So it's more that, the bus rides and the enjoyment of that.*

Vasil's view is not surprising: if the very thing fans seek is a sense of community and togetherness, it is no wonder that a player would most miss community in one of its most authentic forms, the team. Yet, the adulation of fans is also something he misses in his daily life, whether he thinks about it consciously or not:

> *The reason why I don't miss the game as much right now is because I'm still involved in the game. So I think it's just as satisfying. The only thing is you don't get the recognition sometimes of being a professional hockey player. The highlight, and all the fans being around you. You're not as popular. But you know, it's just as satisfying being on the ice, being with hockey players, being in the sport.*

Although Vasil feels he was right to end his career at the point he did and is satisfied by his new career, he still misses "the fans" and being "popular."

Even James, who displays a general distaste for the culture of spectatorship surrounding professional hockey, somewhat grudgingly acknowledges the satisfaction he derived from playing in front of a crowd: "From time to time, you kind of miss the attention, just being the centre of attention out there, everyone knows who you are. But other than that, no, I don't really miss it."

Not all of the players I interviewed found it difficult to recover from playing in front of an adoring crowd. Luc, for instance, became inured to the experience; he does not miss playing for the fans. Although Luc acknowledges that it was exciting for him initially, familiarity dulled that rush to the extent that he no longer even thinks about playing in front of spectators:

> No, no, I've done enough. It's pretty cool when you start your career, the first few games. I remember, when I went to college, it was the first time that I was really playing constantly in front of crowds of five thousand people and then you get to the NHL and it's fifteen, twenty thousand people. I mean, at first it's pretty special, but eventually, you don't even think about that.

Chris actually feels immense relief to no longer be the focal point of the imagined community of fandom:

> I never liked it, to be honest with you ... I don't miss it. I still have anxious dreams ... It's been years since I've played hockey and I still wake up terrified that the game's about to start but I can't find my skates. Or, I get on the ice, but I can't find my footing ... It has nothing to do with my minor hockey experience where you pull in parents, you don't pull in crowds, or the CIS [Canadian university hockey] experience, where you pull in friends and maybe a few people who just like hockey in the area, and they're watching ... The reason I can tell is the colours of the jersey and the socks I'm wearing in these dreams and, so I don't miss it, because for me, that was actually almost a hellish experience, to be honest with you. Some people love the crowd and they thrive off of it ... I don't like judgement based on people who don't know me ... the crowd comes to judge you. They're not coming to meet you and make an educated judgement based on your personality and everything. They're coming to see how you perform and ... you either are something great, or you're nothing, you're a plug ... They all love the stars and then there's the rest. And the rest are interchangeable ... When you score, and you hear the crowd, yeah, you miss that, that's for sure. The roar of when you actually do something good in front of the crowd, so people who are good and successful, I'm sure, will miss the crowd. The ones who just kind of go around and once in a while you'll get a goal and you get that small experience every now and again or do something well, then, yeah, you're pumped up.

For Chris, it was taxing to constantly be confronted by judgement from a crowd, which felt unjust because it was based on a tiny sample of performance and nothing else. Then, too, there is the notion that most players are "interchangeable," generic, and soon forgotten. This is something he was aware of even at the time. Chris does acknowledge the power of the crowd to infuse a player with energy and meaning in celebration of his feats. In a sense, what he is talking about is a dualistic experience of playing in front of a crowd: it elevates or erases. Either way it is dehumanizing, for even the elevation puts players on a pedestal, far above the capacities of individual human beings.

DO OR DIE

The emotional consequences of performing athletic social reproductive labour, particularly the transition from being the vessel for the meaning of the imagined community to being discarded, is one aspect of the cost of this work to athletes, but it is far from the only one. As we talked about before, injury is another devastating consequence of this form of labour. Injury has a variety of dimensions and it comes to shape the experiences of athletes during and after their careers in both intellectual and physical — often inextricably linked — ways. Remember that the players I interviewed for this book were not selected because they had a history with injury. The fact that injury is such a central part of their experience as professional athletes confirms the ubiquity and structural necessity of injury to professional sport.

For players, injuries have an effect even before they occur, provoking anxiety about what might happen to them any time they set their skates upon the ice. Injury could mean the end of a career and the loss of earning potential and a role as the centre of meaning. It also could mean the loss of physical prowess, a fundamental element of the athlete's identity. Lawrence talks about how much the threat of injury haunted him during his career:

> In my case, all the time, because I was a fighter. So every guy that I fought, whether he was a lefty, a righty, I was always worried that if I get hit the wrong way and get knocked out, get my jaw broken, you know, my eye socket broken, and I'm going to be injured for a long time, that means they bring another guy up to do my job. If he does good, I don't have a job anymore. So for me, every game.

One can only imagine the psychological toll of this constant fear of being hurt and losing one's job. This is something players endure throughout their careers. Lawrence and Sean describe how this persistent fear was heightened every time they witnessed a serious injury to another player:

> **Lawrence:** *The Malarchuk [injury] especially. I was a kid watching that in Buffalo, and funny enough, I was coaching with a former captain of the Leafs who played in that game and he said that the third period was the worst period of hockey that anyone played because no one wanted to engage ...*
>
> **Sean:** *No one wanted to engage after, it was a very stalled game. No one was hitting anybody, skating away from checks. For the fans it couldn't have been very fun to watch.*
>
> **Lawrence:** *Yeah, no, and that's what happens when you see something gruesome.*

This exchange reveals the stakes for players of professional sports like hockey. After witnessing the dreadful injury, players were unable to shake an awareness of their own mortality and vulnerability. Although Sean described this event as fluky, as something "that could have easily have happened playing ball hockey as a kid," he suggests something different here: a heightened consciousness shared by the players on the ice that this is the risk they all take. Further, this discussion is one of the few in which a player makes a direct connection between the sacrifice of the athlete's body and the interest of fans. Instead of arguing that no one should have to play in such circumstances, or appealing to the humanity of spectators, he says that "for the fans it couldn't have been very fun to watch." Implicit here is a concession that the players play and endure fear and pain to produce "fun" for the fans. In playing it safe after the injury, the players failed to perform their designated role.

Lawrence's comments on the psychological toll of violence and injury in professional hockey are chilling. They demonstrate the constant emotional sacrifice he was forced to make to prove the high stakes of professional hockey through physical violence. The accompanying fear of injury and failure completely undermined his ability to take satisfaction from his work:

My NHL career was a blur. The road to get to the NHL was memorable. I call it "the journey." Once I got there, it was believe me, it was a nightmare. Because it was a nightmare to stay there, it was a nightmare to fight, it was a nightmare, everything, it wasn't fun. In the summer time, I'd be at my cottage and August would come and I'd say, "I'm about a month out from bare-knuckle fighting." How much fun is that? So here I am, supposed to be enjoying the off-season, and I'm sitting there going, I was on pins-and-needles not even sleeping. First exhibition game was against Philadelphia. Already knew I got three fights in that game. If I don't do well, I'm not making the [team]. How much fun is that? You live it every minute.

Lawrence powerfully refutes the common-sense narrative that playing professional sport is a dream everyone should aspire to and feel grateful to achieve. Instead, he recasts the experience as prolonged emotional abuse, in which he was forced to anticipate the "nightmare" of having to subject himself and others to physical violence in front of thousands of onlookers.

Other players also concede the toll of thinking about and fearing the possibility of injury. In Vasil's case, the fear was of losing his job and getting "sent down ... to a lower level, and that's happened many times. It's happened to me and it's happened to other [goaltenders]" who have "given an opportunity for someone else to step in":

No you can't [sighs], you try not to [think about injury] but yeah, there's, I pushed it aside sometimes because you have no control over it, but definitely, it's in your mind, for sure. It's probably one of the top things in your mind that you think about every day, of course.

Vasil's comment is particularly interesting coming from a player who started out explaining that injuries were not a significant concern for him because of his position as a goaltender. But he later acknowledges that the prospect of being hurt is with a player constantly. Sean was also perpetually worried about getting hurt, especially sustaining head injuries:

Anything with my head. I remember going to the bench lots of times too and, just, when I would take a hit, and they'd say, "hey, you okay?" ... I used to always say, "Just check the eyes. How's the head?" That's all I ever cared about, because I wasn't playing at a level where millions and millions of dollars were at stake. You're playing at a thing where you're almost, I don't want to say paycheque to paycheque, but pretty much you were, and if you took that away, the whole mystique of playing pro, or minor pro, which you always wanted to do, that could be taken away from you pretty quick if you're showing that kind of stuff.

It is worth highlighting his comment about the difference in the levels of professional hockey. For the player at the lower or semi-pro level, the implications of injury are even more disquieting, for there is less infrastructure and patience allotted to recovery. To be hurt is, in a very real sense, to lose one's job. Although the consequences of injury may be steepest at the lowest levels, they remain significant at the highest. Luc worried about opposing players deliberately attempting to injure offensively oriented players like him: "It is something you are very conscious about."

Perhaps unsurprising given the code of masculinity that governs violent sports such as hockey, fear and anxiety about injury are not limited to pain, suffering, or even employment. Darin talks about the humiliation connected to injury:

Darin: *Well I think that you've just got to put yourself in our shoes. I mean, if you were to walk outside tonight in front of twenty thousand people and square off with a big guy, I'm sure you'd have fear about getting injured … It's no different for us.*

Nathan: *And was that fear a question of humiliation in front of the fans? Was it about losing your livelihood?*

Darin: *Humiliation, getting hurt, losing your job, letting your teammates down.*

Darin lived with the constant fear of being humiliated in front of thousands of people. He was acutely aware that the nature of his work was to provide entertainment for spectators and was similarly conscious of the implications of that — the fact that he would be reviled and discarded for failing to fulfil his role.

Although athletes across the spectrum of professional hockey, from semi-pro to the NHL, from goaltenders to scorers, experience emotional distress at the prospect of being injured, this is particularly heightened for enforcers. Both Lawrence and Darin demonstrate the remarkable strain of knowing that they were compelled to sacrifice their bodies each and every time they took the ice. It may appear that these players play a role that is incidental to the game itself, one that renders their experiences exceptional rather than exemplary, but this view fails to account for the context of the economic dynamics of pro sport. Professional hockey is a game played for a particular purpose: to generate profit. In order for professional hockey to be profitable, it must engender fandom; it must create the illusion of inherent meaning and purpose. The construction of the imagined community of fandom relies on the illusion that the game is something more than a game. This is where the enforcer enters: by engaging in gladiatorial combat on behalf of his team, the enforcer validates the sport itself as literally something worth fighting for. This violence makes the sport meaningful for the fan on the profound level of identity. Thus, the enforcer is the ultimate social reproductive labourer in the sphere of professional hockey and, as such, he bears the greatest burden, both emotional and physical, of this work.

Nearly every player I spoke with suffered some form of injury over the course of his professional hockey career, in most cases at least one that was severe. Cataloguing the specific injuries paints a profound picture of the pervasiveness of injury in professional hockey, including injuries to the body and to the head (concussions). Vasil says that injury is a fundamental part of professional hockey:

> *Being a goaltender, I think there's a chance of injury that's a lot less compared to as a player. I think hitting from behind for a player was the biggest concern for me watching players that I played with. The game is at just such high speeds that anything can happen. But being a goaltender, just pucks being shot at you, there's no real risk of injury. The equipment was great too as well. But most of my injuries had to do with my shoulders or knees or hips or stuff like that rather than the real big ones that players can face a lot more than goaltenders.*

As Vasil says, the speed and nature of the game create situations that inevitably lead to injury. Thus, injuries must be understood as an inherent part of professional hockey, not something that is incidental or even particularly avoidable. He expands on this:

There's nothing you can do about it. There's players hurt ... if you look at an American League roster or ECHL [East Coast Hockey League] roster or even, sometimes, NHL rosters, there's thirty, forty players at times that are moving up and down because of injuries and there's nothing you can do. I can go through a season without getting an injury at all and then, you know, there's a season where I went through where I had a couple of injuries, but you cannot, at that speed and that level, you cannot stop injuries from happening.

Injury in professional hockey is the reality all players must accept. Though the equipment and role of goaltenders protect them from most injuries, even for them, as Vasil explains, injury is a part of the game:

My injuries were mainly my hips because of a goaltender that goes down to his knees and gets back up, so we do a lot of that and you've got to stretch a lot to make a save and then the majority of your movement that you use from your hips and there's tons of goalies that I've played with or have seen playing that they have a lot of problems with goaltending is hip injuries.

Although goaltenders are not subject to the contact-based injuries that most hockey players face, the nature of their role leads to a consistent form of bodily harm: hip problems. This is hardly a minor issue, as when these players age they will likely be confronted with increasing mobility difficulties.

Other players also take injury for granted as part of their occupation, despite its obvious significance to their lives and livelihoods. Lawrence lists his most memorable injuries: "Broken back. Shattered heel. Two shoulder operations. I had, I think, fifteen operations through my career. You know, many concussions. Yeah." It is striking the way he recounts the list, almost as if he is entirely disinterested. He states the fact that he had "fifteen operations" as if it is unremarkable. He does not find it necessary to elaborate on the fact that nearly every part of his body was subjected to devastating harm over the course of his career. Sean has much the same attitude: I took a stick in the eyeball in a training session and it tore the retina and I had to get surgery on that to take care of that." This is a rather grievous injury, yet he glosses over it as if it was insignificant; he merely had to "take care of that." As with Lawrence, Sean frames surgery as customary and everyday. Curtis also endured a wide variety of injuries, including a career-ending knee injury:

> Curtis: *I separated both shoulders, broken nose ... I had a bulging disc in my back, and that was it prior to the knee injury.*
>
> Nathan: *Would you say that you ever experienced concussions over the course of your career?*
>
> Curtis: *Oh yeah, sorry, yeah, yeah, you don't consider those injuries, do you? At least, we didn't, but yeah, I had four diagnosed concussions and likely suffered more that just weren't diagnosed or I just didn't address.*

The extent to which injury is actually assumed by players to be an inevitable part of their occupation is betrayed in the way that Curtis says, "that was it" after a litany of significant injuries an average person would be horrified to experience over a lifetime. For a professional hockey player, this is a basic job requirement. In fact, a further comment from Curtis on concussions suggests that even traumatic head injury is considered by players to be a basic expectation of those who labour in professional hockey: "Oh, that was just the norm. Every player went through it, I mean, there's, I would doubt that there's any player that finished the game without at least a couple of concussions." As an overall assertion of the place of injury in the game, this is a pretty remarkable statement. For non-goaltending players, head trauma is understood to be a sacrifice demanded of all players who set foot on the ice.

Luc reveals the incredible amount of pain he was forced to endure in recounting his experience with injury:

> *All kinds of injuries. ... One year, I got my jaw broken. A guy hit as I was trying to stay in the line-up, playing with a guard on my helmet that would allow me to play even if I had a broken jaw. I got hit a few more times during the year and ended up breaking my jaw, or re-breaking it twice ... When you play with a broken jaw and your helmet has this big thing around your face to protect*

you, well, obviously everybody knows that you are playing hurt. And back then, people were not worrying about the hits to the head, concussions, and stuff like that. So obviously, if you have your jaw broken three times in the same year, it's because you got hit to the head three times. Believe it or not, those three times that I got my jaw broken, the only thing that happened was one two-minute penalty [laughs] ... So the other times that I got hit, players did not even get penalized. So that's part of the frustrations that come with that. And the dirty hits and the dirty slashings, and all that stuff, there's nine of my ten fingers that have been broken ... And I have never missed a game because of broken fingers. So again, it's just an example of what players go through ... You play with broken ribs where you have a tough time breathing and stuff like that. So yeah, there's all kind of things that you go through and you battle through and that people don't really know about.

This is an incredible catalogue of injuries, particularly given that they are tolerated to the extent that they typically do not warrant censure for the offending party. This violence is not incidental to the sport. The tacit sanction of violent tactics and behaviour are logically consistent with the fact that professional hockey must have high stakes in order to entice fans to invest meaning and then finances into the game. For players like Luc, this means that they must constantly endure pain and harm to their bodies in the course of their labour — working conditions that would not be tolerated in any other occupation. This is another revealing instance of the hidden cost of this social reproductive work beyond typical exploitation: the actual suffering experienced in the day-to-day course of doing this work.

Luc goes on to recount his experiences with concussions:

I would say, between six and ten in my career ... Well, there's four times, I believe, it was diagnosed. I remember the first one that I really recall was when I was in my first training camp ... and got hit behind the net and just felt a big shake, and back then, people did not even worry about that. You had a concussion, but it was treated like, "Okay, you got [laughs], you got hit hard, and we'll keep him on the bench a little bit and if he doesn't feel right, we'll get him undressed." And, that was about it. There was no follow-up, not

much of the, you know, the big caring that should have been done
... You get on the plane, you go at high altitude after the game, and
the only thing they tell you is, "Can you get your wife to wake you
up a few times during the night." [Laughs] Which is pretty funny
when you really think of it.

Concussions were so commonplace and such little care went into protecting him from the consequences of them that Luc can only resort to humour at the absurdity of the situation. It is impossible to guess just how much harm these concussions have caused him up to this point in his life and will cause him in the future. Darin also speaks at length about his experiences with injury, especially head injury:

Darin: *Yeah, I suffered many concussions. I suffered a broken orbital*
bone where they had to put a plate underneath the eye. A broken
tibia and fibula in my ankle, which put me out all year. And then
a tendon on my right, or sorry, a tendon on my left thumb that was
off the bone and they had to put it back on.

Nathan: *How aware of concussions were you at the time? What*
kind of impact did they have on you?

Darin: *Zero. I had no idea. No idea. It was more of a, you didn't*
feel well or you were sick. But you went out and played again, right
away. So we didn't, there was no protocol for getting knocked out
back then.

Nathan: *So you never missed playing time for a concussion?*

Darin: *Not until my last fight.*

Nathan: *And were they ever diagnosed as concussions, even as they*
sent you back out there?

Darin: *I think I had one that was diagnosed, maybe two. But I had*
a hundred and some pro fights, right? So ...

Nathan: *Wow. And how many times would you, if you had to*
guess, obviously it's just a guess, how many concussions would you
guess you had?

Darin: *Well, there's different grades, but I was told probably around*
seventy-five grade one concussions.

Darin speaks of this number of concussions in a remarkably matter-of-fact way. Indeed, his tone indicates the amount of concern and support offered to players who experienced severe head injury during the period of his career. Yet this is an astounding and deeply disturbing revelation. It is impossible to overstate the level of harm his body was subjected to during his professional hockey career and how little regard was paid to this fact as it was occurring. It is difficult to imagine a more profound illustration of the toll this has upon the athletic labourer.

While most of the players I talked with demonstrated a relatively high degree of equanimity on the subject of injury, this does not mean the injuries had little overall impact on their lives. Rather, it shows the way that athletes must condition themselves to endure the physical and psychological challenges of injury during their careers, given that they are a fundamental element of their work. It would not be possible to pursue a lengthy career as a professional hockey player if one were not able to cope with the challenges of injury. This equanimity does not mean that injuries did not have tremendous emotional consequences in the lives of the players, both during and after their time as professionals. Players are compelled to push their bodies to the point of injury in order to make the imagined community of fandom real and meaningful, but in doing so they sacrifice their physical and emotional well-being. They literally must become another person, another self — one that has less physical agency and less psychological acuity (a result of concussions) in order to reproduce fans in the manner capitalism requires. This is the level of exploitation that professional sport is accountable for.

In Lawrence's comments about the specific nature of the injuries he experienced during his career, he seems to take the harm done to his body in stride. But the fact that he perceives his injuries as unexceptional does not mean that he was emotionally unscathed by the damage he endured:

> *Well, I remember, one was, it was the All-Star break. Our farm team was short players, so they asked me, they didn't tell me, said, you know, "Would you go down and help out?" So as a team guy, I said, "Yeah." So we were playing [out East], back-to-back games in [the East] over the All-Star break. Now, the NHL guys all get a break. So being a good team guy, I went down. The second game,*

okay, was a Saturday night. I was leaving on a plane Sunday morn-
ing to come back to [my NHL city]. I was on a breakaway and [an
opponent], actually a friend of mine, dove out, and I stepped on
his stick. I was going head-first, full-blast in the boards and I spun
around just at the last and hit my feet first [claps] and shattered
my heel. I'm going back to the NHL, I was out most of the rest of the
year, I was out. So talk about devastation, here I am going down
to help the farm team, being a Good Samaritan, and I go down
there and end my season on an injury, on a fluke play ... Oh, I was
sick. Because, the problem was, it's so hard to get to the NHL. And,
here I am, not being sent down, I was asked, would you go help us.
[Management] asked me, I was like, "Of course I'll go," even though
I didn't want to go, because everybody's going to Vegas. So I went,
and it was ... devastating.

The story speaks to the emotional impact of injuries. The damaged body is "devastating" because it is connected to an entire livelihood and identity and comes in service to a larger project. He was playing because he felt it was the right thing to do, and because there was employment pressure, not for himself. It is also worth highlighting that he was hurt by his friend accidentally. As in so many of these stories, injuries are a necessary by-product of the game, not something exceptional. Perhaps most importantly, he vividly recalls the precise circumstances of his injury, including the player who was involved. This is despite the fact that he has difficulty with memory on a daily basis. The mere fact that this memory is so distinct to him after so many years suggests how important the moment was in his life. The details are enshrined in his memory because the emotional impact upon him was too great to forget.

Darin is similarly able to conjure up the specific details of suffering a traumatic injury:

Darin*: My ankle ... Yeah, when I hit the net it had to go one way or*
the other. I looked down at my toes were pointing to the right, my
foot was to the right ... I was on a breakaway and the guy turned
me and I fell down and put my feet up on top of the goalpost and
their goalie was the one that actually said something about it. I
was in shock, I didn't really see it or feel it for the first few seconds,
anyways. And then, uh, yeah, after that I was in complete shock ...

And they had to saw the bottom of my boot off, the skate, because it was too swollen to get off. And then rushed me to the hospital and put, I think it was, nine or ten screws into a plate ... You're not sure if you're going to play again. That's the biggest thing. That's any athlete's fear is having an injury like that and not coming back and being able to perform. So that was the biggest thing.

Nathan: *And would you say that you experienced a really significant amount of that kind of emotional or psychological distress as a consequence of it?*

Darin: *Oh yeah. For sure. Yeah.*

Darin is reluctant to delve into the precise nature of his feelings, but even this somewhat indirect response provides a window into how traumatic an injury like this is for an athlete. He fears for the end of his career and the loss of everything he has worked for. Moreover, he recalls the precise details of his injury, from the way it came about, to the treatment he received afterwards, right down to the specific thoughts passing through his mind at the time. Curtis too is able to recount in detail the occasions on which he suffered serious injuries, including the devastating injury to his knee that ended his career:

So I was playing [a home game and] was chasing the puck, made a quick turn, I got checked, slightly, from behind and it just happened to be the way I fell. It wasn't a vicious hit, it wasn't a brutal attack, it wasn't anything dirty, it was just the way that I fell. My leg was under me when I fell over and went over on the knee the way that you're not supposed to and blew everything out ... I remember afterwards, in the change room, and being given the news that all this damage was done, they're going to have to do surgery. I wasn't upset, I wasn't pissed off, I wasn't scared or anything. It was just, "Okay, well, surgery tomorrow and then we'll start rehab and we'll just carry on." It was just part of the deal, because being around change rooms for so long, there's always guys on the medical table dealing with something and I just kind of felt, "Okay, this is what I'm gonna have to deal with," and I didn't, I, maybe, fully understand how bad the injury was. Just, the way they explained it was, "Okay, we're going to do some surgery tomorrow and you'll be ready for

training camp next year." And, so "Alright, let's just get going here."
That was basically it.

The calmness with which he received news of the injury at the time is striking. Clearly, harm to the body is so normalized for professional athletes that even traumatic events can be portrayed as within the realm of the everyday. Indeed, players often downplay the emotional impact of injury. This is exemplified by the matter-of-fact way Sean downplays the devastating injury to his eye:

It was just more an annoyance, where you just constantly have to go through it and they couldn't find anything and then, eventually I went to a second specialist and they said, "Your retina was tearing apart." So the same guy who did Brian Berard's surgery did mine and, fantastic, unbelievable. But there's still, it looks like, when I'm looking through some water, that's the way I see out of my eye now. So it's okay, but it's not perfect, but it doesn't affect my, I don't think it affects my life at all.

Although Sean acknowledges long-term implications — he continues not to see clearly out of that eye — he vehemently denies that it affects his life in any way. Perhaps this is because it really does have no affect on his life. Or perhaps the trauma is simply easier to reconcile this way.

Unlike Curtis and Sean, Luc speaks at length about the difficulty of experiencing injury:

Today, looking back, obviously [those injuries had] a major effect. You are marked, you know what I mean? It is something that will obviously mark you as an individual. Not that you'll start playing scared, but you will be playing with having experienced that. It's just major. It's just common. When something like this happens, you'll play and think about it, you know?

Although Luc goes on to say that he is primarily talking about the impact his injuries had on him psychologically as a player, the language he uses here invites a somewhat broader reading. He says that his most critical injury "is something that will obviously mark you as an individual … it's just major." Injury has a serious impact on a player's identity as an athlete and as a person. It is also worth underlining that fact that he goes out of his way to say, "It's just common." In his mind, this is not a unique experience:

> *Well, you just, it's something that you don't want to happen again. So if you play, and you're skating down the ice with the puck, and you come to a certain place where you previously in your career got hurt badly, you don't want that to happen again, you know what I mean? It's like, one time, at centre ice, got hit knee-on-knee, and got ... a deep bruise fractured knee, you end up missing eight weeks of play. The next time you skate through the centre ice, it's just something you will look for, in case there's some idiots that are coming to hurt you knee-on-knee again ... So it's, yeah, it's not that you play scared, it's that you play with, in the back of your head, with memories of something bad that happened.*

The distinction Luc makes between playing "scared" and what he is experiencing is interesting beyond the simple fact that he is defending his masculine integrity. He describes feeling as if the injury was internalized as a part of his identity. He is not worried it will happen again; he is unable to shake the memory that it has happened before. He carries that with him in everything he does, especially athletically. This is how it has marked him.

The sacrifices of the athletic labourer cannot be measured according to the physical and emotional trauma suffered during a career alone. Most players express varying degrees of regret about their careers as professional athletes because of the consequences they experienced after their careers ended. Although they may not say that they would have done things differently, they do suggest that there were many aspects of the experience they would have liked to be different so that their post-career life might be more fulfilling. This shows the permanent nature of the sacrifice these men make. They give up something of themselves that they can never reclaim so that the spectator can receive a temporary revitalization. But since the revitalization is only temporary, it is incumbent on other athletes to constantly perform the same sacrifice in order to reiterate the meaning and significance of the game. Because the construct of sport and fandom is artificial, it can never be permanently validated.

Lawrence is candid about the long-term implications and consequences to his quality of life:

Lawrence: *There's nights I didn't even know where I was. I got in a fight on a Friday night, I got hit so hard that I was concussed, and I didn't remember anything until Tuesday. I ended up having two more fights that week and then actually scored two goals, and it all came to me Tuesday where I'm going, "What?" And I realized there was a problem. So when it was to do with the brain, then you're going, "Okay." I didn't realize it back then, because I just played through it.*

Nathan: *How many concussions would you say you probably had during your career?*

Lawrence: *Documented, eight.*

Nathan: *And that's at a time when they weren't documenting nearly as many.*

Lawrence: *Yeah. So who knows, with all the fights I had, and the hits, and stuff. I couldn't tell you.*

Although he is willing to accept the harm done to the rest of his body, he admits that the damage to his head crosses the line. It is poignant and instructive that the head injuries he suffered actually caused him to miss out on the pleasure he would otherwise have taken from a week in which he scored two goals (an anomaly for a player with his role on the team). The consequences of his injuries only worsened in severity after he retired from his career:

Lawrence: *Well, my broken back bothers me every day. My three hand operations, if you look at my hands [shows his hands], all my ligaments and three joints, and my elbow had major elbow surgery, so if I move my elbow the wrong way it hurts. My shoulder, if I turn my shoulder the wrong way it hurts. You know, hernias ... anywhere that there's been a knife on you, you feel it. Yeah.*

Nathan: *Do you think about that a lot?*

Lawrence: *Well, when I'm doing things, yeah. Because I don't want to re-injure it. When I'm working out here today, there's certain things I can do and certain things I can't do.*

Although Lawrence was willing to play through injury and says that it was worthwhile to have done so, it is also evident that he has suffered as a consequence. The professional athlete's body is scarred by the years of playing. To play is, ironically for someone who devotes his life to the optimization of physical capacity, to give up the possibility of complete physical well-being. Lawrence goes on about his experience with concussions:

> Well that's what bothers me because ... there's little things, and this is the best example I can use: I forget if I brushed my teeth or not. So I'm licking my teeth, and I'll go back to see if my toothbrush is wet. So there's little things that are happening where you are going, are the long term effects sinking in from the headshots. So that does kind of scare me a little bit. That does make me think. Because, my memory's not as good. I used to have a great, I could remember anything, and now, I'll have people come up to me that I should know ... I had a guy come up to me at a game last night, eh? ... Honestly, all day long I know him, I don't even know who it is. He goes, Lawrence, it's [name] from roller hockey." I go, "No kidding, how you doing?" And that's when I kind of got a bell going on. There's no way I should have forgotten who that was. So those are the little things that you're going, "Okay, normally that wouldn't happen," right?

Lawrence is not the same person he once was. He once had a vivid memory; now he fumbles to recall basic acquaintances and, more disturbingly, even to remember if he brushed his teeth only moments before. This is not the only consequence of Lawrence's career in professional hockey:

> Take fighting out of hockey. I've been saying it for five years, because the headshots, from punches, getting hit by these guys, people don't realize the damage it's going to do. I watch the UFC [Ultimate Fighting Championship] and I go, "These guys are not going to be able to think when they're later." The amount of headshots they take in training and these fights, they're going to be brain-dead later in their lives ... Well, you look at some of the guys who committed suicide. You know [names a player he knew], he ended up hanging himself, being drunk. And it was a lot to do with his health, it has a lot to do with some personal issues. But I look at him and say,

"Why would he have taken his life?" With a beautiful family, he had money, and I do stem it to, like the football players, to brain trauma and not feeling well. And, it was like the football player who shot himself and left a note ... Duerson ... He said, "I can't live like this anymore." Right. "I can't live like this anymore." And, the guy, Junior Seau. These are, these are situations where you're struggling so bad in life that you're willing to take your life.

Head injury is life-altering. This is what Lawrence sees when he looks at athletes across different sports and his former teammates. The toll of physical play is the inability to appreciate "a beautiful family" or "money." It is the inability to lead a complete life. It is, in the most extreme cases, the inability to continue living at all. This ultimate sacrifice — the sacrifice of the sense that it is possible to endure life itself in the aftermath of a professional hockey career — is something players tend to keep to themselves:

No, no. You never talk about it. I contemplated suicide before, but I was on drugs and alcohol and I was in the worst part of my life until I cleaned it up. But I do know that going on with depression and probably the head trauma and all that, I was close to taking my own life. I just didn't know how to do it. So ...

Even for a player like Lawrence, who was able to move on with his life, suicidal thoughts and drug and alcohol use were direct consequences of his experience with professional hockey. He explains further:

My post-career was terrible because I went into a black hole of drugs and alcohol and almost dying. And then, for the last six years I've been clean. I cleaned my life up after basically losing my life, if you will. So my post-career was terrible. My post-post-career has been great. It's been the best part of my life. Apart from having my three kids, this has been the most peaceful part of my life ... I was this professional hockey player that had money and everything and all of a sudden it comes to an end. What am I going to do? And this is what the problem is with so many players. Where are you going to go? What are you doing? And next thing you know, you lose your marriage, you lose your family, you lose your money, you lose everything, you lose your self-worth. And what you'd rather

do is just die. You're just like, "I'm worthless." Because you're up
here [gestures with his hands] and now you're so far in the hole of
feelings and depression that it's not worth being here. My kids don't
even need me here because I'm worthless.

This is a stark account of the emotional crisis that follows being the
focal point of meaning for thousands of fans. Injury and the accompanying lack of physical agency are part of this, but only part. Another part
of it is inherent to the act of performing this sort of social reproductive
labour itself. When the athlete is no longer the vessel for the meaning
of fans, he comes to feel as if he has no "worth" whatsoever. Chris also
talks about players being "pushed, and pushed, and pushed and found
themselves with nothing but addictions at the end." The full extent of the
athlete's sacrifice is this loss of identity and sense of self. For some, this
loss is too much to endure.

James asserts that the harm caused by injury and concussion are pervasive and generally not worth enduring, but "it depends where you're
playing, right? If you're making millions of dollars, yeah, for sure, it's worth
it … [if] you make a couple hundred bucks a week, what are you really
doing it for?" But he thinks it is different for head injuries: "That'll affect
you for a long time. If you're still waking up with headaches five years
later, then you're probably gonna regret it, but if you went through it for a
year, got your insurance money, then you're probably okay with it." James
focuses on the money more than most of the players interviewed, rather
than the prism of the meaning. If players made a significant amount of
money, it was worth it. If not, it wasn't.

For some, the long-term consequences of athletic labour are more
physical than psychological, although the physical and mental are inextricably linked. Vasil speaks of the way that physical damage accrued
initially during his hockey career has taken an increasingly significant
toll on his health with the passage of time:

I hurt my shoulder in my fourth year of professional hockey. I kept
playing through it and I actually injured it more. I had surgery on
it. But now, being 39 years old, compared to when I was 24, I'm
having a lot more pain through it now than when I played. So when
you're 24 years old and you're young, injuries don't mean anything
to you. You just want to play hockey. Now that I'm 39, I realize,

wow, maybe I should have [taken] some time, some more time off, because of my future, and, you know, doing stuff around the house or with my kids. I've got four kids now, you're lifting them, there, you can feel the pain still, right, so ...

Indeed, one reason why players might be so willing to play through pain is that they don't fully understand how much of an impact it will have on them down the road. For Vasil, the most significant cost of professional hockey for most players is the long-term effect of head injuries. Although he didn't contend with this as a goaltender, it is something he witnesses amongst those he played with: "I've played with *many* players that have had really bad concussions that still affect them today." This basic point was frequently repeated: myriad former players suffer from the effects of head trauma received during their careers. Vasil elaborates:

It happened quite often. Now, obviously, it's talked about a lot more than back when I played. I'm sure that there [were] many more concussions that nobody really said anything about, talked about it. But it would happen, yeah we would have guys, fighting's a big thing in hockey and talked about, and [sighs] there's been many guys where they get knocked right out in a fight. And, that's pretty much a concussion, you can guarantee that. And I've been involved in my eight years of hockey, I've seen seven to ten guys get knocked right out, lying out on the ice. So there's ten concussions right there. And it affects people's lives. I've seen players retire after three, four years because of concussions ... I've been told by many players that they still have their dizzy spells and whatever their problems are. But yeah, I've had many players tell me that, it still affects them now today after, you know, ten years. It's probably been ten years since I've played professional hockey and so ten years later, they're still having problems with it.

Vasil views the post-career experience of former head trauma, described earlier by Lawrence, as unexceptional. Because violence is inherent to the game, it is difficult for those who participate to avoid experiencing damage to their heads that lingers in many cases for the rest of their lives. Is it worth it? Vasil is ambivalent:

[Sighs.] I say yes, just because hockey players, they love the game, they love to play and I just think, I have friends that were construction workers, and they have injuries too, so you know, was it worth it? Yeah. I loved playing the game, obviously, and had fun doing it, so I think it was worth it, yeah … You don't want to be hurt, obviously, of course. But I met so many different people, had lots of friends, it opened up a lot of doors for me, so obviously nobody wants injuries, but my injuries are, I guess, a lot more minor than some other players. Maybe somebody else would tell you that had the bigger injuries with concussions and stuff like that, they'd probably say a different thing.

While Vasil feels his own experience was worth the cost, it is difficult for him to justify the more extreme forms of harm inflicted on the vast majority of players.

Although Luc's experience is less traumatic than some of the others discussed, he too deals with long-term physical consequences to the injuries he suffered as a professional player:

Luc: *Say I have to go shovel the entry in winter, and stuff like that, I do have back pain and sometimes shoulder pains or … When I go do cross-country skiing, I do other sports now … I don't play hockey anymore, but it gives me the chance to do other things and sometimes I do have to deal with back pains, or shoulder pains, or neck pains and stuff like that, and obviously that is directly caused by what happened throughout my career.*

Nathan: *Do you feel that those kinds of pains, the reward of playing and the salary you received made it worthwhile, or do you have some regrets in the big picture?*

Luc: *Well, no, that's the part of the, when you play hockey, you know that you'll have to deal with it. It's something that you should agree to. The only regret that I have is that … instead of playing through injuries, many times, you should just be smarter, or people should not put pressure on you as a player. It's tough because when they're paying you a lot of money and the fans are coming there to see the high-profile players and you're one of them, they want to see you in the line-up. But when you're hurt, when you're badly hurt, I think*

it's just smarter to leave you aside for a couple games and to fix
you up the right way. And, later on in your life, you don't have to
deal with soreness and with back pains coming back all the time.

Luc begins from the premise that players have consented to the physical costs of the game, but he nevertheless returns to the point that he was
compelled to play when he was hurt, and that there have been lasting
physical repercussions he regrets. Indeed, he is physically unable to continue playing hockey in his post-career life because of the accumulated
damage to his body. He also makes a link between having to play through
injury and fans' expectations to see players play, which led management
to ensure that they did.

The long-term effects experienced by Luc are relatively minimal, for he
does not list head trauma among his complaints. The same cannot be said
for Darin, who played through many concussions: "I don't regret anything
in my life. I've learned to say, 'Hey, this is my course, this is the path I went
down.' Do I wish they had a protocol back then? Yeah, sure. But I don't
regret it." He copes with his experience by framing it as his "course," "the
path [he] went down." That he feels the need to do this suggests that he
finds it difficult to reconcile what he went through. He wishes "they had
a [concussion] protocol back then" because concussions are among the
injuries that still trouble him:

> **Darin**: *Well, my ankle, very, very stiff. Not a lot of movement,*
> *not a lot of mobility in it. And then, obviously, [small pause] the*
> *concussions have a part to play too.*
>
> **Nathan**: *How do you experience the consequences of the*
> *concussions?*
>
> **Darin**: *You know, the difficult stuff. Memory loss, tension head-*
> *aches, that kind of stuff, I mean it's [long pause] … I don't know*
> *how to put a finger on it, but …*

The ankle injury and concussions are obviously things Darin will
have to deal with for the rest of his life, but it's difficult for him to speak
about the effects of the concussions. He hints that he endures significant
hardship by referring to "the difficult stuff" when describing symptoms
and then begins to itemize that difficulty before retreating onto the safer

ground of ambiguity. Evidently, the sacrifice he had to make as a professional player is something that he must struggle to reconcile today. The emotional strain of this struggle becomes still more apparent:

> **Nathan:** *More generally, do you find that you ever talk much to other former players about their experiences with injury, concussions, is that something that comes up in your life?*
>
> **Darin:** *No.*
>
> **Nathan:** *Is it the opposite? Is it something that people do not speak about?*
>
> **Darin:** *I don't want, I don't like to rehash any head problems that I had or any injuries. I'm trying to move on with my life. And, when you're in the middle of playing hockey, you're so consumed with injuries and your health and now I'm just happy to not have to fight anymore and be a good father.*

Darin is reluctant to expand, other than that he is "trying to move on" and doesn't "like to rehash any head problems." But he is "happy to not have to fight anymore." Despite these difficulties, he concludes that his career was worth the hardship: "It depends on how you define injury. For me, yeah, but for some guys that have to get their hips replaced or are constantly burdened with major concussion symptoms, no, fuck no." The fact that he defines his career as personally worthwhile certainly speaks to the power of the meaning he attaches to the game. However, he is not willing to make a universal statement about the applicability of his experience. The profanity he uses to describe the experience of others suggests the possibility that he relates to them. Indeed, this is a general trend in the interviews: players often seemed more comfortable discussing the trauma of others rather than themselves. This indirect approach seemed to liberate many to speak more freely. For players socialized to believe that they had attained the height of human experience as professional hockey players, it is evidently a considerable struggle to grapple with the ongoing suffering they are still enduring. Perhaps because this was something that did not fit into the narrative they had been sold as children and because the investment had already been made and could not be reversed, it is too difficult to stare for long directly at the full extent of their sacrifices.

However, some players are able speak openly about the trauma caused by the injuries suffered in professional sport. Curtis is candid about the effects of injury upon his life:

I'll need a knee replacement because the last surgery or last check-up I had, my knee is very arthritic because of the rubbing, bone on bone. The shoulders will pop out every once in a while, and I have to do some exercises to get them back in. My back aches regularly. The first thing I do in the morning is I take pain medication and I'll follow it up with probably pain medication later on in the day, depending on how I'm feeling, but everything hurts [laughs]. When the weather changes, I'm like the old man on the rocking chair, I can tell when the weather is gonna turn bad just because the way my joints are feeling. So it does affect how I, I can't run, so I'm limited physically in what I can do, so there's no quick sports like basketball or tennis or any of those kind of things. Biking is fine, swimming is fine, I still skate occasionally, but I can't perform, obviously, like I was, or like a younger man would. But to me, the biggest issue that I deal with is pain … [The concussions] affected my memory. I need to write everything down, otherwise I will forget most tasks and if somebody tells me something or they want me to do something, I tell them either send me an e-mail or I have to write it down, otherwise I'll forget certain things. You know, I'm very good with numbers, I can remember numbers, I can remember phone numbers and locker combinations and all that sort of stuff, but details or conversations that I have with people or names and so on, I think it has affected my memory on those things.

Like so many others interviewed, Curtis views his experience as broadly representative:

Most guys who leave the game will have something that they're dealing with today and as the years go on it increases, meaning the older I get, the worse the pain gets, so I think that for most guys, there's something. I know that when I get together with the boys every once in a while, the conversation turns to, "So how are you feeling?" You know? "What are you dealing with?" Very few guys actually come out of the game with no injury or no lasting effects on their body.

Earlier Curtis described how much he loved the game and how big a fan he was before he ever became a professional player. Yet this is how he now views the game:

> *The only thing I watch, I very rarely watch a full game, it might be on TV or something, but I very rarely will follow a team. I'm not a fan of the game, but I do cheer when, if it's playoff time or if it's the Olympics or something like that, those are the only games that I'll watch. Regular season or the first part and the playoffs, I tend not to care.*

After a career of injury and mistreatment at the hands of management, the institution around which his life was once organized has lost most meaning and value for him. This is the ultimate indictment of professional hockey as a business fuelled by the sacrifice of players. Curtis does not even seem to have the energy left for rage. This is not a wilful boycott so much as a genuine loss of interest and enthusiasm. He simply does not care about hockey anymore.

Although some players tend to regret the sacrifices they were compelled to make during their professional hockey career, others remark that the sacrifice was worthwhile. This is, of course, important and contradictory. It reveals the power of the meaning produced through the games and the symbiotic relationship between spectators and players. The meaning that fans take from the game elevates those who play it to the status of heroes. This is a form of validation and valorization. Players come to believe that the game is a meaningful end in itself, and this contributes to their willingness to make the sacrifices that in turn fuel the belief of fans in the meaning of the game. The effects of this complex process are apparent in some of the players. Darin discusses the extent to which he was aware of fans during his career and the feeling of fulfilling his dream of playing professional hockey:

> *It's not necessarily more on the ice, more when you're on the bench, having time to take it all in … You're playing in front of twenty thousand people. That was every kid's dream, making it to the NHL, so what I tried to do is, every game, at least once, look up in the stands at all the people that were there and sort of tell yourself that you made it.*

Darin internalized the notion that playing in the NHL was the height of meaning and purpose long before his actual ascent to the league. Looking into the crowd at all of his admiring supporters reinforced and validated his sacrifice on the ice; it had a higher purpose. This no doubt legitimized the risks he took, both physically and emotionally, on behalf of the team.

The powerful effects of this ideology are exemplified in Lawrence's remarks. Even though he is damning about the tremendous toll exacted by this form of labour, he says that it was all worthwhile:

> That's what we signed up for, that's what your dream is. So people say to me, "Knowing now the long-term damage of fighting, what it did to you, would you do it again?" Of course I would. To play in the NHL is a dream. At nineteen, twenty years old you're doing it all day long, every day. Even, ... if they said to me [now], "You get to go play in the NHL, but you've got to go fight this guy, this guy, this guy five nights in a row," I would do it just to say that I had played in the NHL. That's, the, it's the hardest, making the pro league, NFL, NBA, is the hardest thing to do for an athlete. The percentages to get there are very small, so if you asked somebody that, they'll do it all day long. So would I do it again? Yeah.

After everything Lawrence has said about his experiences with drug addiction, suicidal thoughts, permanent memory loss, and a damaged body, not to mention the perpetual anxiety he suffered throughout his career, he still settles on the fact that it was worthwhile. This points to the incredible power of the ideology around sport for young men. Professional sport is framed for them as "the hardest" thing out there to achieve, an accomplishment that validates itself. It produces athletic labour as "a dream" mediated by a feedback loop through fandom: "The percentages to get there are very small, so if you asked somebody that, they'll do it all day long." "Somebody" refers not to some athlete, but to *anybody*. The meaning invested by "anybody" (for which, I think, we can read fans, for they are ubiquitous in the life of the athlete) is what justifies his own willingness to sacrifice himself.

Lawrence is not alone. Sean is similarly resolute in his assessment that a career in professional hockey was worth all that it cost him, saying he would "do it again ten times over." Despite an eye injury that has never fully healed, he feels grateful to have had a career even as a semi-professional player. Perhaps most remarkably, given the harrowing saga of the mismanagement of the knee injury that ended his career, Curtis too testifies that his sacrifice was justified:

> *No, it's just part of the deal that you take the good with the bad. I don't think anybody would change it or at least not in the conversations that I had. I don't regret anything, I don't think any of the players regret dealing with the issues they're dealing now. I think for some of us, yeah, maybe they would have handled it a little bit differently. I think concussion treatments, I think most guys are starting to realize maybe they should have been handled differently, but as far as bones and knees and joints and whatnot, it's, those things, you're not going to change too much of that. But from the conversations I had with players, nobody regrets having to go through anything that they're going through.*

Professional sport is a business predicated on producing meaning for fans. But for players like Lawrence and Curtis, it is equally true that in a reciprocal way the investment of fans in turn influences the attitudes of players. Because players are raised and live their lives in a society that idolizes the game they play as one of the most prestigious imaginable professional pursuits, they themselves internalize this rationale, and this is what induces them to sacrifice themselves. On this level, professional sport is as much about meaning as money for fans and players. Players condition fans by performing athletic contests as do-or-die spectacle, and fans condition players by investing their identities in that spectacle, in the process solidifying the meaning associated with it. The work of athletes reproduces not only the identities of fans, but also through a feedback loop, their own understanding of the world as athletic workers. The existence of sacrifices that players make on the ice implies to fans and players alike that such sacrifices could only exist in the service of something inherently meaningful.

Performing social reproductive athletic labour is complex. Not all professional athletes experience the work they perform in the same way, and their ideological investments are not necessarily founded on the particularities of their own experiences. Yet, with that said, the toll of athletic social reproductive labour is great. Because athletes must be willing to subject their bodies to enormous harm in order to validate the meaning of professional sport, they experience manifold consequences that shape their post-career lives. Indeed, the very act of serving as a repository of meaning for legions of spectators is one that seems inherently fraught with the possibility of emotional letdown and potential personal crisis. This crisis is only compounded by the physical damage suffered by most players over the course of their careers, especially the head injuries, which have the potential to radically alter — or even prematurely end — their lives.

Given the ambivalence articulated by players, it is impossible to render any final verdict on the legitimacy of professional sport. Yet, there is a cost to this labour that is not typically named or acknowledged. This cost is not incidental but rather at the very heart of the dynamic that makes professional sport viable as a business. It is only in the sacrifice of the athlete's body that fans can fully come to extract the meaning from professional sport that they so desperately need within the context of neoliberal capitalism.

CHAPTER 6

RE-IMAGINING SPORT AND SPECTATORSHIP

This book discusses the exploitation experienced by athletic labourers and the enduring appeal of sport to spectators, and shows how they are inextricably linked. It is impossible to understand either athletic labour or sports fandom without viewing them as part of a larger system in which each plays a part. That system is capitalism.

The purpose of capitalism is to produce surplus value, or profit. In order for capitalists to generate profit, they must exploit the labour-power that is supplied by workers by extracting more labour from the worker than they pay for, keeping the surplus value for themselves. Making profit is the ultimate goal of the system, and workers are essential as the means to that end. Although capitalism and professional sport can exist without each other, they have proven to be both compatible and mutually beneficial. In fact, professional sport has come to play an increasingly significant role in the capitalist system.

As an economic system, capitalism makes tremendous demands of its workers in terms of the amount of labour it requires and the types of human social relations it imposes. Capitalism requires workers to sell their labour for a wage, a process that alienates them from the fruits of that labour. This transforms their relations with other people into relations of exchange and competition. Since a fully realized human existence is one that is shared with others in a collaborative and collective life, capitalist relations of exchange and competition are dehumanizing. This has obvious negative repercussions for the worker, of course, but it also poses risks for the sustainability of the system itself. If capitalism were to utterly exhaust the working potential of its labour supply by draining it physically and emotionally through the deadening effects of alienation, it would be left with no labour to exploit and thus no ability to generate profit. This is why capitalism requires a mechanism for the reproduction of its labour power, both in terms of the actual bodies and minds of its current workers and in terms of future generations of labourers.

Unlike productive labour, social reproductive labour does not produce profit directly. Yet it is no less essential, for without this type of labour, productive labour and profit (surplus value) are not possible. Historically, social reproductive labour was primarily unpaid domestic labour done by women, who worked to sustain both the men who laboured in the productive labour force and the children who would replace them. This social reproductive work involved both physical and emotional elements, because it needed to ensure that workers could literally subsist as labouring bodies, but also that they could endure the emotional deprivation of the alienation from their work and from other human beings. Social reproduction is no less important to capitalism today than it once was. What has changed is that, in some instances, it has become paid work (inside and outside the home) and thus part of the productive economy.

This is where professional sport enters the picture. The labour of professional athletes is a form of social reproductive labour because of the way that it provides an emotional renewal for fans. Spectators who experience isolation and alienation in their day-to-day lives come to sport seeking meaning, connection, and community. Professional sport provides a foundation upon which an imagined community can be built. In consuming the spectacle of professional sport and participating in the accompanying imagined community of fandom, spectators experience the social reproduction they require in order to be productive capitalist workers. In this way professional sport has become a significant reproductive mechanism for the capitalist system itself.

Just as capitalism relies on professional sport, professional sport relies on certain features of capitalism to sustain its own business model. The spectators who flock to professional sporting events are a market of people in search of community, and professional sport offers that community through the labour of its high performance athletes. Athletic labourers provide the framework for imagined communities of fandom, for it is their bodies that must bear the weight of the almost limitless desire that spectators foist upon them. The imagined community — the collective fantasy produced for fans by professional sport — requires that athletes sacrifice their bodies completely. It is only through this sacrifice (actual or potential) that the imagined community of fandom becomes solidified as something tangible and spectators become willing to spend their money on attendance at sporting events, cable television and online streaming packages, memorabilia, and other associated commodities and revenue-sources.

Interviews with eight former professional hockey players and eight fans provide us with a window into their unique experiences of participation in sporting culture and allow us to examine the ways in which broader social, economic, and political phenomena are lived by people every day. Former players consistently draw linkages between the economics of professional sport and the harm and exploitation athletes experience in the course of their work. Nearly every player understood that it was their job to make fans care about the games they played and that if they failed to do so, the construct of professional sport — and their livelihood — would collapse. This is not altogether surprising given that players come to experience that the sausage of professional hockey is made out of their bodies. The views of spectators on the subject of the business of sport are notably different. Rather than acknowledging that the meaning and pleasure they derive from watching professional sport is based on the destruction of athletic bodies, most spectators seem relatively, even wilfully, oblivious to this reality.

This suggests that a form of alienation exists between athletes and spectators. Athletes are aware that spectators are often unable to empathize with the brute reality of their occupation. Luc remarks: "The effort and the sacrifice to play is out of this world and it's something that people don't know." This failure to recognize the level of "sacrifice" made by players "creates misunderstandings ... and, that's normal. If people are not aware of that, how can you be sympathetic to the athlete you're watching if you don't know?" Curtis makes a similar point: "[Fans] see the athlete, they see them on the field or on the ice, and they expect that performance to be there every night and sometimes the player is dealing with something, it could be emotional, but most times it's physical, that would limit them from performing at their best." What spectators don't seem to fully internalize is that players are human beings too, beset with similar challenges, including those posed by a commodified existence within capitalism. Thus a form of alienation exists between the athlete and the spectator. The spectator comes to sport as a member of an individualistic society seeking a sense of community through the investment of meaning in the bodies of athletes. Yet, this very act of investment transforms the athlete into a tool or instrument, a means to an end, rather than a fellow human being in the sought-after community. Athletes understand this process as it occurs, because it is a process that denies them their humanity by transforming them into something both more (the heroic vessel) and less (the discarded failure) than human. Spectators, on the other hand, largely remain oblivious to these destructive elements of the imagined community of fandom and the ways in which it alienates them from the very people it is constructed upon — the athletes.

AN OPIATE FOR THE MASSES?

Does this mean that sports spectatorship is inherently dehumanizing and therefore unredeemable? Is it an "opiate for the masses," a form of what some political thinkers have called "false consciousness?" Georg Lukács, a Hungarian political theorist of the last century, said that consciousness of belonging to one economic class or another could be either true or false depending on whether or not people comprehend the nature of the existing economic system and the political activism that would be required to improve the conditions of that system.[1] In the case of the industrial working class, true consciousness would be an awareness that capitalists exploit them and an understanding that revolution against the capitalist system is both possible and the only way to improve it. False consciousness would involve some confusion over these conditions, whether it be a mistaken belief that capitalism is natural and necessary or that it benefits the working class. This is not to say that Lukács thought false consciousness simply affected ignorant dupes. Rather, as Ron Eyerman, a sociologist at Yale University, argues, all individuals and groups in a capitalist society experience some form of false consciousness, regardless of class, particularly in the sense that they see the market economy to be the natural and normal form of relations between human beings.[2] The important point, however, is that some classes benefit from this false consciousness, while others do not. Athletes demonstrate a significant awareness about their material conditions (the money they can make, the prestige they have) and their position in corporate capitalism. Spectators appear to experience false consciousness in that they take an entirely instrumental view of athletes, who become for them objects through which they attempt to achieve community and renewal. The athlete is seen not as an ally in a struggle to produce a more humane society for all, but rather as a tool that can be used to temporarily alleviate the dissatisfactions living in capitalism produces. It is this objectification of the athlete by the spectator that some might call false consciousness. Seeing another person in this way fails to comprehend the truth of a shared humanity and the potential of collaborative effort for change; this failure serves the capitalist system well. Could an alternative understanding provide a space for imagining how sports spectatorship might be transformed within capitalism — what possibilities and alternatives it offers to resist the system?

Like Lukács, Antonio Gramsci considered the question of false consciousness, in his case developing the concept of hegemony. Gramsci argued that social relations peculiar to capitalism have become naturalized and normalized to the extent that they are simply understood as common sense for most people; this becomes the hegemonic, or dominant, view.[3] In the case of professional sports, most spectators see athletes in an instrumental way that allows them to vicariously find meaning in their lives. This (alienated) form of social relations is normalized within a system that always seeks to maximize profit above all else. Yet Gramsci said that hegemony or false consciousness is never absolute or universal (nor does it need to be for the system to successfully reproduce itself). Raymond Williams writes: "Thus, we have to recognize the alternative meanings and values, the alternative opinions and attitudes, even some alternative senses of the world, which can be accommodated and tolerated within a particular effective and dominant culture."[4] Pockets of resistance can and do exist within — and are even are tolerated by — a dominant system. This observation is vital because it means there may be political agency and a desire for social change even in contexts where false consciousness is pervasive. If resistance can exist within a hegemonic culture, then it can be nurtured and eventually blossom to challenge the system itself.

Therefore, we should not merely dismiss those who relish the exploitative world of professional sport as victims of false consciousness. Rather, we should look for alternative visions of spectatorship that suggest new, more humane ways of participating in sporting cultures. Paul provides such an alternative when speaking about the level of responsibility or guilt he feels for athletic injury. Unlike the other spectators interviewed, he makes a direct connection between athletic sacrifice and the needs of spectators:

> *If the hype to win is such that they feel the responsibility to get out there even although their instincts tell them that they are actually, could be putting themselves and their long-term life, in jeopardy. Why would you take steroids, and all of that? I do feel a measure of responsibility. Because, I don't think anybody does things which are detrimental to their body, unless ... there's also a lot of weight of responsibility of the fans to, "Get out there, you bum." And, so I don't think about it a lot, but I have to say that I do feel some measure of responsibility ... when teams encourage athletes to do what's unhealthy for them they're doing it because they think it's good for business, i.e., the fans want them to do it.*

Although this is just one voice among many, Paul shows that a passion for sports spectatorship does not preclude the possibility of empathy and connection between players and fans. Mason is perhaps the most outspoken of the fans about the pleasure he experiences from and the admiration he has for athletic sacrifice. When he talks about the role of injury in the game, he waxes poetic about the passion and toughness of professional hockey players and the way that their sacrifice endorses his own investment in the game. However, when his discussion turns to a player he was once personally acquainted with, the tone of his comments radically shifts. Suddenly, his preoccupation is with the horror at the potential harm that would befall Steve Stamkos as a consequence of his injury: "Watching that, you really understand how dangerous the game is, and what you put your body through and sacrifice for this entertainment, for themselves as well as for the fans." The fantastical dehumanization of the athletes becomes at least tenuous in the face of the humanity of his former acquaintance. Paul's ability to see the connection between violence and the economics of sport and Mason's dismay at the harm experienced by a player he knew betray cracks in the hegemony of the imagined community of fandom and social reproductive athletic labour. With this example in mind, the question becomes how these cracks might be splintered wider.

FACE-TO-FACE ENCOUNTERS

Guy Debord writes that "spectacle's job is to cause a world that is no longer directly perceptible."[5] Spectacle — the endless distractions of postmodern life — is useful to capitalism because it produces distance between people. This distance can cause us to lose the sense that we are connected in a fundamental way to other human beings. As a society, we have increasingly come to view one another through the remove of screens. Other people become objects to be consumed for (fleeting) personal gratification. Nowhere is this truer than in professional sport, where most spectators interact with players only through their television screens or, at best, from dozens of metres away in colossal stadiums. If there is any potential for a different professional sport to emerge, what is required is bridging the gap between spectators and players, for example, through face-to-face encounters. Such encounters are actually not unheard of in the lower tiers of professional sport. In fact, for Sean, who played professionally in England, face-to-face encounters with spectators were an everyday aspect of his existence as an athletic labourer:

> It was huge. After every home game, you'd have to go to the supporter's club. And, supporters that helped with meals on the road, and stuff like that, and they would do things, you know, for your apartment, or your flat in England. You needed a TV, they were always there to provide stuff for the team. So after games, there was always a lot of interaction with the supporters. So lots of times you would go in there, you would have a quick beer with them, and you'd do other things ... the school visits, and all the other stuff you'd have to do, right? ... I loved it ... And then there was, especially in the second division ... in smaller towns, before you get on the road, we might go up to, and most rinks would have a bar or pub-type, so you'd go out and maybe grab a couple beers, especially on a Sunday when your weekend was, you'd play Saturday, Sunday most nights, and on a Sunday, if you were on the road, you'd go up to the bar and grab a couple beers to take back on the bus, or whatever, and so they would come up and talk to you ... For example, there was this one time we were playing and I thought I scored, so I threw my hands up. But the puck didn't go in, so every time I got the puck, they all went, "Yay!" [mimes

throwing his hands up], thinking I was scoring. And then you see them after, and it's just fun, it's entertainment.

In Sean's experience, small-scale, lower level professional sport does not foster the same alienation as the top level pro leagues. Unlike so many of the players I interviewed, who experienced aggravation and alienation in their encounters with fans, Sean took obvious satisfaction from his more direct interactions. These experiences included sharing meals and drinks and even reciprocity such as the gifting of furnishings and televisions. This does not mean that Sean lost an awareness that his labour *was* labour, and he had no illusions about the exchange nature of his relations with fans, but he was still able to at least partly resist the commodification of his interactions. This is because instead of simply producing community *for* spectators through his own sacrifices, Sean actually participates in a community *with* fans. Although Sean received considerably less remuneration and celebrity from his career in professional hockey than nearly every other player interviewed, it is he who seems to have drawn the most satisfaction and least anguish from his career.

The face-to-face elements in Sean's experience of professional hockey offer a glimmer of possibility for there to be less alienated forms of athletic labour and spectatorship more generally. For philosopher Emmanuel Levinas, a face-to-face encounter does not entail merely *looking* at the other (as in the typical spectator-athlete dynamic of professional sport). The look involves knowledge, and knowledge is, naturally, associated with power. To look at a person is thus to objectify that person as a "character," constituted only by "everything that is in one's passport, the manner of dressing, of presenting oneself." The spectator gazes at the athlete from afar, reducing him to an object or tool that can satisfy his insatiable desire for meaning and community. A more ethical form of relation, for Levinas, on the other hand, "is discourse and, more exactly, response or responsibility."[6] In other words, it is through dialogue/conversation with another that we come to ethically acknowledge their humanity. The spectator must not merely look at athletes but rather must listen to what athletes have to say about the nature of their experience. By acknowledging the humanity of another through face-to-face dialogue, we are also confronted with the ethical necessity of taking "responsibility" for the well-being of that person. In the moment of authentically listening to the athlete, the spectator must also accept responsibility for the harm the athlete suffers. Sean shows us that it is possible for this sort of dialogic face-to-face encounter to exist in the world of professional sport. In doing so he allows us to imagine how a different sort of professional sport might be possible, one in which the labour of athletes would provide pleasure and even the foundation of community for fans without requiring the sacrifice of the athlete's body. Through face-to-face connections, fans might experience the empathy currently lacking in the imagined community of fandom and athletes might be able to participate in the communities they labour to create.

Because this vision may appear far-fetched in the world of large-scale, corporate professional sport, I finish this book with an example of possibility drawn from the experience of the highest performance professional basketball players in the world. During the 2011 National Basketball Association lockout and the summer that preceded it, we witnessed encounters between elite athletes and spectators that looked very different from what we have come to expect in the era of spectacular sport.* This was a conscious, player-led movement away from the big business, big spectacle model of professional basketball. Instead, games were organized that featured the best players in the world (including Kevin Durant and LeBron James) in urban communities in the United States for affordable tickets that could be obtained on a first-come, first-served basis. These events were held in small arenas and playground courts, and they broke down the distance between athletes and spectators.[7] Andrew Sharp describes the experience of attending these events from the standpoint of spectators:

> Vendors hawked mixtapes and Len Bias t-shirts in the aisles of the grandstand, teenagers sold homemade food on the baseline, and everyone froze every few minutes with the latest jaw-dropping dunk. Security was minimal if not invisible, but it never mattered. Maybe out of respect for Rawls [a local organizer] or just respect for the event itself, nobody abused the privilege that came with being ten feet away from NBA superstars for two hours. Or maybe

---

*   The lockout, which technically began on July 1, 2011, delayed the start of the 2011–12 NBA season from November 1 to December 25 and shortened the regular season from 82 to 66 games. The primary issue at stake was how league revenue would be divided between owners and players.

nobody wanted to risk getting kicked out, missing out on their chance to see the spectacle first hand. In any case, the community event showcased a community that used basketball as an excuse to come out and party together peacefully.[8]

This example shows the potential in spectatorship for a different kind of community connected to sport that is based on the face-to-face encounter. Spectators, in this setting, were face-to-face with both athletes and each other. They were part of the same community. This coming together, particularly in the context of systematically exploited working-class African-American communities, also produces the potential for greater forms of real change.

It is not only spectators who benefit from these dynamics. Kevin Durant explains why he participated in these events: "I just want to hoop ... I do it for everybody back here that really don't get a chance to see me that much. I just want to break the barrier." Later, he adds, "It feels good to go into different hoods and show them my game ... People respect it."[9] This brief, even passing, line is illuminating. It suggests a mutuality of exchange at these events. However, it is "respect" that is being exchanged rather than cash, and this leaves Durant feeling "good" rather than exploited or used. Later, speaking of a game at Rucker Park in New York in which he scored 66 points and was "mobbed by fans after a flurry of 30-foot three-pointers," he adds, "It was unbelievable, man ... Just a great atmosphere, people showed me so much love. It was one of the best moments of my life." This is a striking pronouncement given that Durant is accustomed to having success in front of enormous crowds. What is different in this context is the intimacy. He is, in a sense, a member of this crowd, not an object onto whom they are projecting their needs. This is likely a moment that will endure for Durant because it is one he shares with people who will not simply discard him for the next vessel of meaning to come along. It is a community he can always remain a part of. This is the kind of community high performance sport has the potential to build. Forms of sport and spectatorship that can bring athletes and fans together might actually have the potential to disrupt the logic of the imagined community by humanizing the athlete. If athletes come to be seen as people rather than as avatars, it becomes much more difficult to objectify them as mere vessels of meaning. This in turn undermines the possibility of making the sort of imaginative investments imagined communities of fans rely upon. However, this does not mean that *no* community is possible. Rather, it becomes much more feasible to envision a form of athletic community that contains both athletes *and* spectators.

While reducing the distance between spectator and athlete can help facilitate a more humane relation between these two groups, such a change will have a negligible impact as long as professional leagues and teams, rather than athletes themselves, control the means of production in professional sport. Exploitation will always remain a feature of high performance sport as long as athletes must sell their labour to another for a wage. Further, the imagined communities of fandom will continue to flourish as long as capitalism continues to produce an insatiable appetite for community by isolating and alienating its workers. This means that professional athletes will continually face the pressure to provide social reproductive labour. Thus, although a movement towards more face-to-face encounters between athletes and spectators can to some extent mitigate the dehumanization and objectification of professional sport, full liberation from the sacrifice of athletic labour will only come with emancipation from capitalism itself. This is a struggle we must all share in, whether athlete, spectator, or neither.

Of course, there is a role within sport for a challenge to the broader system itself precisely because of the significance of athletic spectacle to capitalism. Both athletes and spectators have parts to play. In the realm of athletic labour, resistance is built into the current model in the form of athletic labour unions — players associations — which attempt to check and limit the power, authority, and exploitative tendencies of management. Athletic labour unions have remarkable potential because the labour of the most elite athletes, unlike most other forms of labour, is not as replaceable through the reserve army of unemployed workers. It is not possible to readily find an alternative supply for the exceptional physical capacities of the most elite professional athletes. Indeed, this potential has been demonstrated even at the college level, where scholarship restrictions place a similar premium on players to that enjoyed by the top professional athletes. In 2015, thirty Black football players at the University of Missouri threatened to cease all football activities unless certain racist conditions on campus were resolved, including the resignation of Tim Wolfe, the school's president.[10] Faced with the loss of millions of dollars' worth of revenue, the university succumbed to the players' demands. Yet, professional unions have not altogether lived up to the potential that comes from the withdrawal of labour. In fact, with respect to the pivotal issue of concussions, the National Football League Players Association has been sued by former players over failure to protect their interests.[11] The reason why athletic labour unions don't live up to their potential is because they are deeply invested in the current model. Their goal is to maximize the workings of the current system for players, not produce a new system. That would be beyond their purpose and scope as presently imagined. This is, to a significant degree, a problem of hegemony and consent; in short, an ideological, not structural, limitation.

This does not mean that there is no room for players to resist in the current system. Ultimately, professional sport is a celebration of athletic ability. The business of sport exists because people want to watch players play. The traditional logic governing North American sport is that sport and politics must not mix, which means that sport has served a spectacular function for capitalism, deflecting attention away from inequality, injustice, and change. Yet, spectator sport is not inherently spectacle. If politics enter the arena, the immense popularity of professional sport can actually create an amplificatory effect. Colin Kaepernick, at the time a quarterback with the San Francisco Forty-Niners of the National Football League, began protesting against structural racism and police violence against racialized Americans by refusing to stand for the national anthem in 2016.[12] By fall 2017, Kaepernick was out of a job — likely as retribution — and the president of the United States was publicly commenting on an escalating wave of on-field protests.[13] Kaepernick's brave and defiant stance reveals the power of athletic resistance. If athletes are willing to put their livelihoods on the line, they have the platform to begin and sustain nearly any conversation they choose, with or without unions, including one about the legitimacy of capitalism and the occupational requirement that they sacrifice their bodies in order to reproduce it.

Yet while athletes have the power to start the conversation, they cannot carry it alone. It is fans who are in the end responsible for transforming the conditions of professional sport — and capitalism. Fans tacitly endorse the current model by spending their money on games. It is only when fans refuse the seductive allure of this sacrificial and spectacular enterprise that professional sport can change. Like players, fans have the capacity to reject the distinction between politics and sport and organize new, until now unimagined, forms of resistance to athletic sacrifice. Maximum potential lies in the solidarity of fans *and* athletes together. The business of professional sport is entirely dependent upon human labour and a market to consume the fruits of that labour. If athletes and fans can unite in the common cause of humane working conditions, inside and outside of sport, there is little that owners of capital can do to stand in the way of radical transformation. For fans, this process begins with acknowledging the full humanity of the professional athlete. This is more difficult than it sounds, for it means giving up the fiction of the imagined community of fandom — the fantasy of collective meaning fuelled by the sacrifice of athletic bodies. It is in this new form of sacrifice — the sacrifice of spectacular meaning and investment — that authentic hope and possibility can be found. There is a place for sport and spectatorship in a more just and equitable society, just as there is a place for art and other forms of leisure and pleasure. That version of sport is one that celebrates both the aesthetic and arduous dimensions of human physical performance precisely because they are the feats of actual human beings. Such a humane rendition of high performance sport may be a means as well as an end. Perhaps, in the cultivation of empathy, compassion, and community between athletes and spectators we can begin to imagine a new form of social relations outside of the dehumanization, alienation, and exploitation of capitalism.

NOTES

Chapter 1

1. ESPN.com news services, "Chris Conte: NFL Worth Early Death," *ESPN.com*, December 17, 2014. <http://espn.go.com/chicago/nfl/story/_/id/12040968/chris-conte-chicago-bears-says-playing-nfl-worth-long-term-health-risk>.

2. Steve Nash, (Facebook status update), November 7, 2014 <https://www.facebook.com/stevenash/posts/10152770496175250>.

3. A.C. Sparkes, "From Performance to Impairment: A Patchwork of Embodied Memories," in J. Evans, B. Davies and J. Wright (eds.), *Body Knowledge and Control: Studies in the Sociology of Physical Education and Health* (New York: Routledge, 2004) p. 165, 168.

4. Quoted in Michael Monette, "Heavy Hitting: Concussions and Safety Law," *CMAJ*, 184, 12 (2012): E641.

5. Julian Ammirante, "Manufacturing Players and Controlling Sports: An Interpretation of the Political Economy of Hockey and the 2004 NHL Lockout," in A.C. Holman (ed.), *Canada's Game: Hockey and Identity* (Montreal: McGill-Queen's Press, 2009) p. 187.

6. Barbara Laslett and Johanna Brenner, "Gender and Social Reproduction: Historical Perspectives," *Annual Review of Sociology*, 15 (1989): 381–404.

7. Evelyn Nakano Glenn, "From Servitude to Service Work: Historical Continuities in the Racial Division of Paid Reproductive Labor," *Signs: Journal of Women in Culture and Society*, 18, 1 (1992): 1–43.

8. Bridget Anderson, *Doing the Dirty Work? The Global Politics of Domestic Labour* (London: Zed Books, 2000) p. 2.

9. For example, Bridget Anderson, *Doing the Dirty Work;* and Anna M. Agathangelou, *The Global Political Economy of Sex: Desire, Violence, and Insecurity in Mediterranean Nation States,* 1st ed. (New York: Palgrave Macmillan, 2004).

10. Benedict Anderson, *Imagined Communities: Reflections on the Origin and Spread of Nationalism* (London: Verso, 1991). The concept that sports fandom takes the form

175

of an imagined community was previously proposed by Rex Nash, "Contestation in Modern English Professional Football: The Independent Supporters Association Movement," *International Review for the Sociology of Sport*, 35, 4 (2000): 465–86, and Chris Stone, "The Role of Football in Everyday Life," *Soccer & Society*, 8, 2/3 (2007):169–184.

11. Paul Gilroy, *Against Race: Imagining Political Culture Beyond the Color Line* (Cambridge, MA: Belknap Press of Harvard University Press, 2000).

12. Arlie Russell Hochschild, *The Managed Heart: Commercialization of Human Feeling* (Berkeley: University of California Press, 1983).

13. Ann Ferguson, *Blood at the Root: Motherhood, Sexuality & Male Dominance* (London: Pandora, 1989) p. 83.

14. Guy Debord, *The Society of the Spectacle*, trans. D. Nicholson-Smith (New York: Zone Books, 1994 [1967]).

15. Benedict Anderson, *Imagined Communities*, p. 7.

16. Carly McKay, Raymond Tufts, Benjamin Shaffer et al., "The Epidemiology of Professional Ice Hockey Injuries: A Prospective Report of Six NHL Seasons," *Br J Sports Med*, 48 (2014): 58.

17. McKay, et al., "The Epidemiology of Professional Ice Hockey Injuries."

18. M.A. Brandenburg, Dale Butterwick, Laurie Hiemstra et al., "A Comparison of Injury Rates in Organised Sports, with Special Emphasis on American Bull Riding," *International SportMed Journal*, 8 (2007): 80, 60.

19. Robert A. Stern, David Riley, Daniel Daneshvar et al., "Long-Term Consequences of Repetitive Brain Trauma: Chronic Traumatic Encephalopathy," *PM&R*, 3, 10S2 (2011): S460–64.

20. J. Mez, Daniel Daneshvar, Patrick Kiernan et al., "Clinicopathological Evaluation of Chronic Traumatic Encephalopathy in Players of American Football," *JAMA*, 318, 4 (2017): 363.

Chapter 2

1. Jean-Marie Brohm, *Sport: A Prison of Measured Time: Essays* (London: Inklinks, 1978) p. 19.

2. Michael A. Robidoux, *Men at Play: A Working Understanding of Professional Hockey* (Montreal: McGill-Queen's University Press, 2001) p. 28.

Chapter 3

1. Edward Galeano, *Soccer in Sun and Shadow*, trans, M. Fried (London: Verso, 2003).

Chapter 4

1. David McNally, *Monsters of the Market: Zombies, Vampires, and Global Capitalism* (Boston: Brill, 2011).

2. Anne McClintock, *Imperial Leather: Race, Gender and Sexuality in the Colonial Context* (New York: Routledge, 1995).

3. Paul Gilroy, *Against Race: Imagining Political Culture Beyond the Color Line* (Cambridge, MA: Belknap Press of Harvard University Press, 2000).
4. Guy Debord, *The Society of the Spectacle*, trans. D. Nicholson-Smith (New York: Zone Books, 1994 [1967]).
5. R.W. Connell, "An Iron Man: The Body and Some Contradictions of Hegemonic Masculinity," in Michael Messner and Don Sabo (eds.), *Sport, Men, and the Gender Order: Critical Feminist Perspectives* (Champaign, IL: Human Kinetics Books, 1990) p. 83–95.

Chapter 6

1. Georg Lukács, *History and Class Consciousness: Studies in Marxist Dialectics,* trans. R. Livingstone (Cambridge, MA: The MIT Press, 1971).
2. Ron Eyerman, "False Consciousness and Ideology in Marxist Theory," *Acta Sociologica*, 24, 1–2 (1981): 43–56.
3. Raymond Williams, *Problems in Materialism and Culture: Selected Essays* (London: Verso. 1980).
4. Williams, *Problems in Materialism*, p. 39.
5. Guy Debord, *The Society of the Spectacle*, trans. D. Nicholson-Smith (New York: Zone Books, 1994 [1967]) p. 17.
6. Emmanuel Levinas, *Ethics and Infinity: Conversations with Philippe Nemo,* trans. R.A. Cohen (Pittsburgh: Duquesne University Press, 1985) p. 85, 88.
7. Andrew Sharp, "LeBron James and Kevin Durant, Spreading the Gospel in Baltimore," *SB Nation*, August 31, 2011 <www.sbnation.com/NBA/2011/8/31/2395040/lebron-james-kevin-durant-baltimore-goodman-league-camelo-anthony>.
8. Andrew Sharp, "Love This Game: The Genius of Basketball's Endless Summer," *SB Nation*, August 22, 2011. <www.sbnation.com/NBA/2011/8/22/2377341/kevin-durant-punishment-goodman-league-drew-league>.
9. Michael Lee, "Kevin Durant Stars at Goodman League, Sets Oct. 1 Deadline for Potential Overseas Decision," *Washington Post*, August 14, 2011 <https://www.washingtonpost.com/blogs/wizards-insider/post/kevin-durant-stars-at-goodman-league-sets-oct-1-deadline-for-potential-overseas-decision/2011/08/14/gIQAnNgPFJ_blog.html?utm_term=.125aaa8b1726>.
10. J. Pramuk, "Missouri Resignations Show NCAA Athletes' Power," *CNBC*, November 9, 2015 <https://www.cnbc.com/2015/11/09/missouri-resignation-shows-ncaa-athletes-power.html>.
11. N. Fenno, "NFL Players' Assn. Sued over Handling of Concussions," *Los Angeles Times*, July 14, 2014 <http://www.latimes.com/sports/sportsnow/la-sp-sn-nfl-players-association-sued-over-handling-of-concussions-20140718-story.html>.
12. E. McKirdy, "NFL Star Colin Kaepernick Sits in Protest During National Anthem," *CNN*, August 28, 2016 <http://www.cnn.com/2016/08/28/sport/nfl-colin-kaepernick-protest-sit-down-national-anthem/index.html>.
13. D.A. Graham, "How Trump Turned Kaepernick's Protest into a Success." *The Atlantic*, September 25, 2017 <https://www.theatlantic.com/politics/archive/2017/09/trump-turned-kaepernicks-protest-into-a-success/540999/>.

INDEX